© 2015 Viva-eBooks All rights reserved. No part of this book may be reproduced or transferred in any form or by any means, photocopying, scanning, recording, taping or by any other information storage retrieval system with the express written per... ... ...d are used without any consent and the publication of the trademark is without permission or backing by the trademark owne... ...or clarifying purposes only and are the property of their respective owners and not affiliated with this document. Viva eBooks ... mentioned in this book. The fact that an individual, organisation or website is referred to in this work as a citation and/or p... ... ...n that the author or publisher endorses the information the individual, organisation or website may provide or recommendat...

This book is sold on the understanding that the publisher and author are not engaged in providing medical, legal or other pr... ... ...he information provided within is for your general knowledge only. The information, advice and strategies contained herein may not suitable for every situation. If you require professional or medical advice or treatment for a specific condition, the services of a competent, qualified professional person should be sought promptly.

This book is designed to provide general information in regard to the subject matter. While reasonable attempts have been made to verify the accuracy of the information provided, neither the author nor the publisher assumes any responsibility for errors, omissions, interpretations or usage of the subject matters within.

Warning on Allergic reactions – some recipes included in this book use nuts or nut oils. These specific recipes should be avoided by:

- anyone with a known nut allergy

- anyone who may be vulnerable to nut allergies such as pregnant and nursing mothers, invalids, the elderly, babies and children

Warning on Eggs – The US Department of Health's advice is that eggs should not be consumed raw. Some recipes included in this book are made with raw or lightly cooked eggs. These specific recipes should be avoided by:

- anyone who may be vulnerable such as pregnant and nursing mothers, invalids, the elderly, babies and children

Warning on Blending Hot Foods and Liquids - Remove from the heat and allow to cool for at least 5 minutes. Carefully transfer to a blender or food processor, ensuring that it is no more than half full. If using a blender, release one corner of the lid, which helps prevent heat explosions. Place a towel over the top of the machine, pulse a few times before processing according to the recipe directions.

Contents

INTRODUCTION

WHY COOK GLUTEN-FREE?

There are a number of reasons why you may want to cook Gluten-Free. These can range from having a medically-diagnosed autoimmune disease through to gluten sensitivity or making a personal, lifestyle choice.

Celiac/Coeliac Disease or Dermatitis Herpetiformis

Celiac/Coeliac Disease and Dermatitis Herpetiformis are both autoimmune diseases whereby eating gluten causes the lining of the gut to be damaged (Celiac/Coeliac Disease) or causes a rash with red, raised patches and/or blisters, most commonly found on knees, elbows, shoulders, bottom and face (Dermatitis Herpetiformis). If you or a family member has been diagnosed with Celiac Disease (as it is called in the US) or Coeliac Disease (as it is called in the UK) or Dermatitis Herpetiformis, you will already know that these are life-long, gluten-triggered autoimmune diseases. The charity, Coeliac UK, estimates that Celiac/Coeliac Disease affects 1 in 100 people, although only 1 in 4 sufferers have had the condition diagnosed, and that 1 in 10,000 suffers from Dermatitis Herpetiformis. In America, over 3m people have been diagnosed with Celiac Disease. These are life-long conditions caused by a reaction to the gluten, which is a protein found in wheat, barley and rye. Anyone who is diagnosed with either of these conditions will need to follow a gluten-free diet for the rest of their lives. Celiac/Coeliac Disease does run in families, which unfortunately means that if an immediate blood relative (mother, father, brother, sister) suffers from the disease, then the chances of also having it yourself increase tenfold to 1 in 10. This disease can develop at any age, even in someone who has previously been able to eat gluten without an issue.

Gluten Sensitivity

In addition to the two autoimmune diseases described above, there is growing evidence of non-coeliac gluten sensitivity. This is when someone experiences symptoms similar to Celiac/Coeliac Disease, but there are no associated antibodies and no damage to the lining of the gut. Currently this is much harder to diagnose. However, it is established medical advice that anyone experiencing these symptoms seeks proper medical diagnosis and is tested for Celiac/Coeliac Disease, <u>before</u> eliminating gluten from their diet.

Choosing to Eat Gluten-Free

Surveys have shown that up to 1 in 3 adults are interested in following a Gluten-Free diet and that interest is growing. In fact, one survey found that 3 out of 4 people who follow a Gluten-Free Diet do so for reasons other than a diagnosed medical condition. Lots of people believe that a Gluten-Free Diet promotes general digestive health and that it reduces toxins in the body.

What About Oats?

Oats do not contain gluten but they do contain the protein avenin, which is similar to gluten. Fortunately, research has shown that it is safe for <u>most</u> people with Celiac/Coeliac Disease to eat avenin. However, there are a very small number of people with Celiac/Coeliac Disease who may still be sensitive to gluten-free, oat products. So, the decision on whether or not to include oats in your diet is something that you do need to discuss with your qualified medical advisers if you suffer from Coeliac Disease. If you can tolerate oats, then they can make a great contribution to a healthy, balanced diet. Oats are an excellent, low-fat source of soluble fibre, which helps to keep a healthy gut. They contain beta glucan which can help lower harmful high cholesterol. As oats are high in soluble fibre, they are slower to digest and can help to keep blood sugars stable. They are a rich, natural source of several essential minerals and vitamins including manganese, zinc and vitamin B1.

However, importantly, if you are able to include oats in your diet, they must be sourced from a certified gluten-free source which ensures that they have not been cross-contaminated with gluten during the manufacturing process.

WHY A GLUTEN-FREE, WHEAT-FREE EASY BAKING, BREAD & MEALS RECIPES COOKBOOK?

If you're reading this book, it's fair to assume that either you or someone you cook for needs to follow a gluten-free, wheat-free diet. However, do you think that gluten-free baking and wheat-free meals can't possibly taste fantastic? Does the idea of wheat-free bread and pastry conjure up images of heavy and unpalatable food? Do you think that eating gluten- and wheat-free means turning your back on all your most-loved recipes? It can be quite tricky ensuring that baking and meals are gluten-free. The typical, modern "Western-diet" relies heavily on gluten-rich products, such as bread and flour. This in itself can be a big enough worry, but on top of that, it can also be ridiculously expensive!

With the rise in awareness of gluten-triggered autoimmune diseases such as Coeliac Disease or Dermatitis Herpetiformis, more and more shops are offering gluten-free alternatives to standard products – but, unfortunately, these come at quite a significant price premium. For example, in my research I found the following:

- that a pack of two Gluten-Free Pizza Bases cost 100% more than the same brand "standard" Pizza Bases

- that the Gluten-Free Victoria Sponge version cost 85% more than the same brand "premium but gluten-containing" Victoria Sponge

Whilst in the UK, gluten-free staple foods (such as bread, pasta and pizza bases) are available on prescription for anyone diagnosed with Coeliac disease or Dermatitis Herpetiformis, it remains the case that there is also much less variety and choice in the gluten-free aisle. For example, in my research, I could not find ready-prepared and gluten-free versions of almost all of the recipes I have developed for my cookbook. So what are you to do if you crave:

- crisp, flaky, melt-in-your-mouth pastries
- light, airy celebration cakes
- crusty, golden, tasty breads and buns
- luscious, decadent puddings and desserts?

My aim with this book is to show you how you can combine readily available ingredients along with a few of my tips and tricks (that help guarantee perfect results), to create much-missed foods to be enjoyed and savored. With my tried and tested recipes, you can create over 50 wheat-free & gluten-free baking, bread and meal ideas.

HOW TO USE THIS COOKBOOK

Which Wheat-Free Flour?

Most of the recipes in this book that call for flour use a ready-blended plain/all-purpose gluten-free flour mix, such as Bob's Red Mill (US) or Doves Farm (UK). There are two main reasons for this. Firstly, these ready-blended mixes are now very widely available in almost all main supermarkets, meaning that my recipes are easy to use wherever you live or shop (although I have also provided some online stores that carry these ranges in the final section of this book, Resources – Gluten-Free Ingredients). Secondly, using just one all-purpose blend is also friendlier on the wallet, especially when you are starting out on cooking gluten-free. As you continue on your gluten-free journey, you can expand your range of gluten-free flours and start to experiment with them. If you are already a seasoned gluten-free cook, then you may have your own gluten-free blend, in which case, please do use this in place of the proprietary brands.

Milly's Tips & Tricks for Perfect Baking

Whilst most of my recipes in this book that use flour are based on ready-blended plain/all-purpose gluten-free flour mix, I do use a few ingredients that have been key to providing the taste, texture and rise associated with perfect bakes. I have spent many years baking and these little tips and tricks will make a much an amazing difference to your finished result. These are:

- Xanthan Gum – this helps improve the crumb structure and reduce crumbling in baked items. It's a natural ingredient that is produced by fermentation of glucose or sucrose. However, this is a product where a little goes a long way. Please use only the amount directed in the recipe, using a proper set of spoon measures, then level off with the back of a knife before adding to the flour mix. Also, do double check that your flour blend does not already include xanthan gum.

- Glycerine (culinary Glycerol) – this really helps baked goods taste moist and is a tip from my experience of baking beautifully decorated celebration cakes such as wedding cakes. It used to be that you had to buy this from chemist or pharmacy, but with the rise in interest in baking, this ingredient is now widely available in small bottles from the home baking section in supermarkets. Again, please measure accurately.

- Cornflour/Corn starch – even if your flour blend includes other starches such as potato flour, please do try following my recipes when they also call for cornflour/corn starch. This is another tip from my baking experience, and helps turn plain/all-purpose flour-blend into flour that has similar properties to traditional pastry flour, which, in turn, gives very light, airy results. Again, please measure accurately.

- Air – some recipes ask you to beat some ingredients really well (often when creaming together the fat and sugar), sometimes for up to 10 mins. This is to add a really important ingredient that doesn't appear on the ingredient lists but is essential to light baking. This secret ingredient is AIR! I hope you don't think I'm trying to insult your intelligence with this tip. However, it is so important to understand that beating air into your mixture (and then taking care not to knock it out again) will, in turn, result in light, <u>airy</u> baked goods. I know it sounds obvious, but it does require a bit of patience not to rush this stage. Just stick the food mixer on and let it work its magic, you'll be so glad you did.

Other Dietary Considerations

Whilst this book is primarily aimed at gluten-free cooking, I appreciate that you may also be concerned about other dietary needs too. Obviously all the recipes in this book are Gluten-Free and Wheat-Free. However, if you have additional dietary requirements or concerns, I have also categorized every recipe into a number of "Free-From" concerns and these are indicated by the following symbols:

Symbols

GF Gluten-Free and Wheat-Free, meaning no gluten-containing cereals including wheat, rye, barley, spelt, wheat germ, nor any processed ingredient containing these.

DF Dairy-Free meaning no milk, cheese, cream, yogurt, butter nor any other ingredient derived from the milk of cows, goats, ewes or buffalos (or any other milk-producing mammal).

NF Nut-Free meaning no peanuts and no tree nuts including almond, brazil nut, cashew, chestnut, coconut, hazelnut, macadamia nut, pecan, pine nut (pignoli), pistachio or walnut nor any processed ingredient containing these. Nutmeg is considered to be a seed rather than a nut, so the ingredients nutmeg and/or mace are classified as nut-free ingredients in this book.

OF Oat Free meaning no oats, oat bran nor any processed ingredient containing these.

V Vegetarian meaning no meat, poultry, game, fish or shellfish, nor any by-product from processing such ingredients. However, Vegetarian recipes may include honey, eggs and dairy. See below regarding cheese.

Ve Vegan meaning no meat, poultry, game, fish, shellfish, dairy, honey, eggs nor by-product from processing such ingredients.

YF Yeast Free meaning no yeast or any processed ingredient containing yeast.

Also, if a recipe does include one or two ingredients that preclude it from being "free-from", where possible, I will include alternative options showing how the recipe can be adapted, for example, non-dairy margarine for butter. Old hands at recipe adapting will already be very familiar with this, so apologies in advance for some fairly obvious substitutions. However, my cook books are bought by a wide variety of readers, but I've included this advice especially if you are either new to cooking for these needs or if you do not regularly cook for these dietary needs and are not used to making such recipe substitutions.

Finally, a note for vegetarians, where a recipe includes cheese but is indicated with the V symbol, it assumes that the cook will use vegetarian cheese if that is required.

Metric vs American Measurements

All recipes are provided in both Metric and American measurements. In order to provide meaningful equivalents, there may be slight "rounding" differences between the two systems, but these do not make a material difference to the overall calorie count. Egg sizes differ between the UK and the US. Most of the recipes in this book are based on UK Large Eggs which is equivalent to American Extra Large Eggs, but the recipe will always advise on the correct egg size.

Both European English and American English names have been given for ingredients where they differ in common usage, for example, Fresh Coriander or Fresh Cilantro.

Standard level spoon measurements are used in all recipes

- 1 tsp = 5ml
- 1 tbsp = 15ml
- A pinch = $\frac{1}{8}$ tsp

Top Tips for Safely Cooking Gluten-Free

Avoid Cross-Contamination

When you first start cooking gluten-free or if you don't keep an entirely gluten-free kitchen (perhaps as other members of the family do eat gluten), it's very important to avoid cross-contamination between gluten-free and not gluten-free ingredients and kitchen equipment. This may sound straight–forward but it really does require diligence and attention to detail. So, when cooking gluten-free:

- use separate chopping boards, breadboards, non-stick pans, cast iron cookware or any other kitchen utensil/tool that is porous or can be scratched or has "joins" (for example, wood handled silicone spatula, wood rolling pin, wood mixing spoons, metal sieve)
- wash all surfaces thoroughly
- thoroughly clean all cooking utensils and equipment prior to use and then keep them separate during food preparation and cooking
- keep cooking oils and condiments separate
- ideally have a separate grill and toaster for gluten-free cooking but if space or budget won't allow, then use toaster bags to keep gluten-free items uncontaminated.

Read Labels on Processed Foods

Gluten can lurk in the most unlikely processed foods, so take care to carefully read the ingredients lists and allergy advice on all processed foods. For example, as well as the obvious items of bread, pasta and granola, some brands of the following ingredient staples can contain gluten:

- some brands of instant coffee
- some brands of stock cubes
- most ready meals
- oats that are not certified as gluten-free

American Vs Metric Measurements

All recipes are provided in both Metric and American measurements. In order to provide meaningful equivalents, there may be slight "rounding" differences between the two systems, but these do not make a material difference to the overall calorie count. However, please follow either the metric or American measures within a recipe, don't mix the two together.

The description of egg sizes also differ between the UK and the US. Unless otherwise stated, the recipes in this book are based on UK Medium Eggs which is equivalent to American Large Eggs. However, each recipe clearly states the egg size required for the recipe (and therefore the calorie calculation).

Both UK English and American English names have been given for ingredients where they differ in common usage, for example, courgette or zucchini.

Standard level spoon measurements are used in all recipes:

- 1 tsp = 5ml
- 1 tbsp = 15ml
- A pinch = $^1/_8$ tsp

Classic Pastry Recipes

Sweet Choux Pastry

Ingredients

- 60g (¹/₃ Cup + 1 tbsp) Gluten-Free Plain (All Purpose) Flour Blend
- 15g (2 tbsp) Cornflour (Corn starch)
- 50g (3 tbsp) Butter
- ¼ tsp Xanthan Gum
- 2 UK Large (US Extra Large) Free Range Eggs
- ½ tsp Natural Caster (Superfine) Sugar

Directions

Preheat the oven 200C, 425F, Gas Mark 7. Line two baking sheets with baking parchment, and then splash with cold water so that the parchment has tiny drops of water on its surface (you don't want it drenched or puddles of water, just a very light spritz). I do this by holding my (clean!) hands under the cold water tap, and then just shaking them over the baking sheets.

Measure out 150ml (½ Cup + 2 tbsp) of cold water into a saucepan and add the butter. Place over a medium heat, fully melting the butter then bring up to a brisk simmer (don't over boil).

Meanwhile, fold a sheet of parchment in half with a sharply pressed fold. Open up and sift together the flour blend, cornflour/corn starch, xanthan gum and sugar straight onto this parchment sheet. This sheet will allow you to very quickly tip in the flour mix when required. As soon as the water/butter is simmering, remove the pan from the heat, pick up the parchment sheet and quickly tip in the flour mixture all in one go. Using a spatula or handheld food mixer, beat together vigorously to form a smooth, thick paste. Beat in the eggs, one at a time, until the pastry is smooth and glossy.

If making éclairs, spoon the pastry into a piping bag fitted with a large nozzle and pipe out the pastry into 12cm/5" stripes, leaving plenty of space around each éclair. For choux buns, transfer a heaped dessert spoon of pastry per bun onto the baking sheets whereas for profiteroles, use a heaped teaspoon. Use a wet finger to flatten any peaks.

Place in the oven and bake for 20-25 mins (éclairs/buns) or 15-20 mins (profiteroles), until beautifully risen, crisp and golden in colour. Remove to a wire rack to cool then fill as desired, such as my Choc & Nut Choux Buns!

Dairy-Free Option: Replace the butter with dairy-free margarine.

Makes: **10 Buns or Éclairs or 20 Profiteroles** Ready In: **30-40 mins**

Choc & Nut Choux Buns GF OF V YF

Ingredients

- 1 quantity of Sweet Choux Pastry
- 100g (3½ oz) 70% Cocoa Chocolate
- 240ml (½ Cup) Double (Heavy) Cream, divided
- ½ Cup Walnut Halves (optional)

Directions

Make the Choux Buns as directed in the Sweet Choux Pastry recipe. Whilst the buns are cooking, roughly chop the walnuts. Place a sauté pan over a medium heat and add the chopped walnuts too toast. Keep an eye on them and cook until the nuts are toasted. Set to one side.

When the buns are cooked, make the hot chocolate ganache. Break up the chocolate into heatproof bowl and add 100ml (½ Cup less 1 tbsp) of cream. Fill a saucepan with enough water so that you can rest the bowl over the pan without the bottom of the bowl touching the water. Bring the water up to a gentle simmer and then rest the bowl over the pan. Melt the chocolate, stirring occasionally (don't worry that the mixture will look grainy whilst it is melting). Once the chocolate is fully melted, beat the chocolate/cream mixture until smooth and glossy. Remove the pan from the heat and set aside, which will keep the chocolate sauce warm until required.

In a clean bowl, whip the remaining cream until thick. Transfer to a piping bag fitted with a plain nozzle. Pierce a hole in the side of a cooled bun and fill with whipped cream. When all the buns are filled with cream, spoon the warm chocolate sauce over each bun (if the sauce has become too thick, simply put the bowl back over the pan of water, return the pan to the heat and warm up, stirring until at the required consistency). Scatter the buns with toasted nuts.

Dairy-Free/Nut-Free Option: Replace the butter with dairy-free margarine. Omit the chopped nuts.

Makes: 10 Buns Ready In: 1 hr

Cheese Choux Pastry

GF NF **OF** V YF

Ingredients

- 60g ($^1/_3$ Cup + 1 tbsp) Gluten-Free Plain (All Purpose) Flour Blend
- 15g (2 tbsp) Cornflour (Corn starch)
- 50g (3 tbsp) Butter
- 55g (9 tbsp) finely grated Parmesan Cheese, divided
- ¼ tsp Xanthan Gum
- 2 UK Large (US Extra Large) Free Range Eggs
- ½ tsp gluten-free Mustard Powder
- $^1/_8$ tsp Cayenne Pepper

Directions

Preheat the oven 200C, 425F, Gas Mark 7. Line two baking sheets with baking parchment (for buns or puffs). If making a choux ring, draw a 20cm/8" circle onto the parchment (trace around a cake tin or plate). Turn the parchment over so that that the drawn side is underneath (but you should still be able to see the circle to use as a template) and line a baking sheet. Next splash the parchment with cold water so that the parchment has tiny drops of water on its surface (you don't want it drenched or puddles of water, just a very light spritz). I do this by holding my (clean!) hands under the cold water tap, and then just shaking them over the baking sheets.

Measure out 150ml (½ Cup + 2 tbsp) of cold water into a saucepan and add the butter. Place over a medium heat, fully melting the butter then bring up to a brisk simmer (don't over boil).

Meanwhile, fold a sheet of parchment in half with a sharply pressed fold. Open up and sift together the flour blend, cornflour/corn starch, xanthan gum, cayenne pepper and mustard powder. This sheet will allow you to very quickly tip in the flour mix when required. As soon as the water/butter is simmering, remove the pan from the heat, pick up the parchment sheet and quickly tip in the flour mixture all in one go. Using a spatula or handheld food mixer, beat together vigorously to form a smooth, thick paste.

Beat in the eggs, one at a time, until the pastry is smooth and glossy. Set aside 2 tbsp of freshly grated Parmesan Cheese then tip the rest into the paste. Beat again to combine.

To make a choux ring, spoon dessert spoons of pastry into a ring on the lined baking sheet, using the traced circle as a guide. For choux buns, transfer a heaped dessert spoon of pastry per bun onto the baking sheets whereas for gougères, use a heaped teaspoon. Use a wet finger to flatten any peaks. Sprinkle over the retained parmesan cheese.

Place in the oven and bake for 30-35 mins (ring), 20-25 mins for buns or 15-20 mins for puffs, until the pastry is beautifully risen, crisp and golden in colour. Serve hot, you can split and fill the ring or choux buns with a hot or cold savoury filling, or simply serve the gougères straight from the oven as they are.

Makes: **1 Ring or 10 Buns or 20 Gougères (puffs)** Ready In: **30-45 mins**

CARAMELISED ONION & GRILLED GOATS' CHEESE CHOUX RING

Ingredients

- 1 quantity of Cheese Choux Pastry
- 200g (7 oz) Goats' Cheese Log
- 2 large Spanish Onions
- 2 cloves Garlic
- 16g (1 tbsp) Butter
- 2 tsp Olive Oil
- 2 tsp finely chopped Fresh Thyme
- 60g (¼ Cup) Mascarpone Cheese
- ¼ tsp freshly ground Black Pepper
- ¼ tsp Sea (Kosher) Salt

Directions

Start by peeling the onions and slicing very finely.

Make the choux ring as directed in the Cheese Choux Pastry recipe. As soon as you have put the ring in the oven, heat the butter and olive oil in a non-stick sauté pan over a medium heat. Add the onion slices, tossing them in the buttery oil and then turn the heat down to low. Leave the onions to cook slowly, stirring frequently until they have turned a deep caramel colour.

Finely chop the garlic and thyme and set aside until required. Slice the goats' cheese into 1cm/½in thick slices and place onto a parchment lined grill pan.

Five minutes before the choux ring is ready, pre-heat the grill to moderately hot. Add the onion and garlic to the onions and cook for 1 min. Place the goats' cheese under the grill for 2-3 minutes, until the cheese has melted and begun to brown. Meanwhile, stir the mascarpone cheese, salt and black pepper into the caramelised onions and turn off the heat.

Remove the choux ring from the oven and protecting your hands from the heat, remove from the baking sheet and split in half using a serrated knife. Place the bottom of the ring onto a warm serving plate, spoon over the creamy onions, then top with the grilled goats' cheese. Finally top with the top half of the choux ring and serve.

Serves: 3-4   Ready In: 1 hr

FLOUR-FREE HAZELNUT SWEET TART CRUST

Ingredients

- 200g Blanched Hazelnuts
- 50g (¼ Cup) Natural Caster (Superfine) Sugar
- 40g (3 tbsp) Butter
- ½ tsp Vanilla Extract

Directions

Grease the tart case(s) and line the base with a circle of parchment paper. It is best to use loose-bottomed tart cases for this crust otherwise it is tricky to remove the delicate crust after baking.

Place the hazelnuts into a food processor and pulse until ground. Melt the butter, and add this plus the vanilla extract and sugar to the ground nuts. Pulse again in the food mixer until thoroughly combined (don't over process, the text should be like very slightly damp sand).

Press the mixture into the base and sides of the tart case, use the back of a spoon to press the base level but you will need to use clean fingers to press into the sides of a fluted tart case. When finished, chill in the fridge to set for 20 mins.

Preheat the oven to 160C fan, 350F, Gas Mark 4.

Place the tart(s) onto a baking sheet and into the oven. Bake for 8-10 mins for individual tarts or 12-15 mins for 1 large tart, until lightly golden. Watch very carefully to ensure that the crust does not burn.

Remove from the oven and allow to fully cool then fill as desired, such as my Hazelnut Crunch & Chocolate Cream Tartlets.

Make this Dairy-Free/Vegan? – Replace the butter with vegan butter or sunflower spread.

Makes: 6 tartlets or 120cm/8" tart Ready In: 30-45 mins inc chilling time

Hazelnut Crunch & Chocolate Cream Tartlets

Ingredients

- 1 qty Flour-Free Hazelnut Sweet Tart Crust
- 100g (3½ oz) Dark Chocolate
- 85g (3 oz) Milk Chocolate
- 300ml (1¼ Cups) Double (Heavy) Cream, divided
- 5 tsp Icing (Confectioners) Sugar
- 1 tsp Vanilla Extract
- 6 whole Blanched Hazelnuts

Directions

Make the hazelnut tart crust as directed in the Flour-Free Hazelnut Sweet Tart Crust recipe, bake and chill.

Meanwhile, set aside in the fridge 1 small square of milk chocolate and break up the rest of the chocolate into heatproof bowl. Fill a saucepan with enough water so that you can rest the bowl over the pan without the bottom of the bowl touching the water. Bring the water up to a gentle simmer and then rest the bowl over the pan. Stirring occasionally, allow the chocolate to melt completely, then set aside to cool.

In a clean bowl, add 180ml cream, plus the vanilla extract and sugar. Whip until it just holds its shape. Fold 1 tbsp into the cooled chocolate to slacken it, then carefully fold in ½ of the whipped cream. Once it is fully incorporated, carefully fold in the remainder of the whipped cream.

Pour the chocolate mousse over the tartlet crust and chill in the fridge for at least 2 hrs. Once it has set, whip the remainder of the cream in a clean bowl until it is stiff. Spread over the chocolate mousse but leave a gap around the edge so that you can still see the chocolate centre. Use a fine grater and grate over the retained square of chocolate. Decorate with the hazelnuts. Serve chilled.

Makes: **6 tartlets or 120cm/8" tart**   Ready In: **30 mins** plus chilling time

SUET PASTRY GF DF NF OF V Ve YF

Ingredients

- 180g (1¼ Cups) gluten-free Plain (All Purpose) Flour Blend
- 20g (2½ tbsp) Cornflour/Corn starch
- 90g (²/₃ Cup) gluten-free Vegetable Suet
- 2 tsp gluten-free Baking Powder
- ½ tsp Xanthan Gum
- ½ tsp gluten-free Dry Mustard Powder
- ¾ tsp freshly ground Black Pepper

Directions

In a large bowl, whisk together all the dry ingredients. Add the suet and use a table knife to mix it in until all the ingredients are well blended. Measure 120ml (½ Cup) of cold water into a jug. Start to bring the pastry together by adding a tbsp of cold water and mixing to combine with the knife. Keep adding a little more water at a time until the pastry comes together into a soft dough. Don't worry about using only part of the water and having quite a lot left over. Precisely how much water you need depends on a number of different factors which Makes: it hard to be exact on how much liquid you'll need. So, just take it slowly, don't add too much water in one go, and you will get to the stage when you have a ball of soft dough, with a few bits of flour/fat left over.

At this point, use clean hands to knead the dough fully together and leaving the sides of the bowl clean. Wrap the ball of dough in kitchen wrap and chill in the fridge for 20 mins. Use this pastry to make steamed puddings such as my Slow Cooker Steak & Kidney Pudding.

Makes: enough to line a 1-1.2L (4-5 Cup) pudding basin   **Ready In:** 30 mins inc chilling time

Note: Suet is a shredded white fat, originally from animal although my recipes use the vegetarian version, which is lower in saturated fat. Although suet is readily available in the UK, the leading brand is not gluten-free. In North America, it is not widely available at all. UK Readers can find recommendations on gluten-free sources of Vegetarian Suet in the Resource chapter of this book. However, an alternative method to create a shredded fat, especially for North American Readers, is to freeze a block of vegetable fat/shortening, and then coarsely grate it to the required quantity. This may sound a lot of fuss, but suet pastry is so easy to make, even if you are someone that normally struggles with pastry, so it is worth the effort.

SLOW COOKER STEAK & KIDNEY PUDDING

GF DF NF OF YF

Ingredients

- 1 quantity of Suet Pastry, chilled
- 215g (7½ oz) trimmed Lamb or Beef Kidney (weight after cores removed)
- 450g (1 lb) Stewing Beef
- 1½ tbsp gluten-free Plain (All Purpose) Flour Blend + extra for rolling out pastry
- 1 Red Onion
- 1 gluten-free Beef Stock Cube
- ½ tsp freshly ground Black Pepper
- ¼ tsp Sea (Kosher) Salt
- 2 tsp gluten-free Worcestershire Sauce
- Sunflower spread for greasing pudding basin

Note: In the UK, the leading brand of Worcestershire Sauce is not gluten-free, although the same brand in the US is gluten-free. UK readers can find recommendations on gluten-free sources of Worcestershire Sauce in the Resource chapter at the end of this book.

Serves: 4 (generously) Ready In: 8-9 hrs

Directions

Peel and thinly slice the onion. Cut the steak into large bite size pieces, removing all visible fat. Trim the kidneys into bite size pieces, taking care to cut around and remove the cores, which should be discarded. Rinse the trimmed kidneys and pat dry on kitchen towel. Combine the meat and onion in a bowl, sprinkle over the flour, salt and pepper and crumble in the stock cube. Toss to ensure that everything is well covered in the seasoned flour.

Generously grease a heat-proof 1L (4 Cup) pudding basin with the sunflower spread. Cut a circle of baking parchment 2.5cm/1" wider than the top of the pudding basin. Prepare a piece of kitchen foil 50cm/20" long. Fold in half to create a double layer and then fold a 2.5cm/1" pleat into the centre. Finally, you need to create a foil "lifter" to raise and lower your pudding in and out of the slow cooker. Take 2 pieces of foil that are each long enough to be place inside your slow cooker with enough excess to create handles. Fold each of the sheets into four length-wise to create sturdy strips. You are going to place one East-to-West and one North-to-South under the completed pudding to use to lift in and out of the slower cooker.

Take your chilled dough and set aside about ¼ to use as a lid. Roll out the larger piece between two well-floured sheets of greaseproof paper into a circle shape large enough to line your pudding basin with a short overlap if about 2.5cm/1" (I measure my bowl and it requires a 30cm/12" circle including overlap). The pastry will be quite "short" ie fragile. If you can transfer it from the sheet of greaseproof into the pudding basin in one go, then brilliant! If it breaks up, don't worry at all. Just patchwork together pieces of rolled pastry into the bowl to line it, pressing with your fingers to join the pieces together to make sure that there are no gaps and the basin is fully lined (in my picture of the finished pudding above, my fully- lined basin was actually a patchwork of about 8 different pieces pressed together to no ill-effect). Once you have lined the basin, roll out the retained pastry between flour-dusted greaseproof papers to a circle large enough to form a lid.

Scatter $^1/_3{}^{rd}$ of the onion slices into the bottom of the lined pudding basin. Add half of the seasoned meat, followed by another layer of onion, then the remaining meat and finally the remaining onion slices. Sprinkle over the Worcestershire Sauce. Carefully add enough cold water to reach almost the top of the filling (take it slowly and don't over fill). Dampen the basin pastry rim and carefully lift over the pastry lid. Press all around to fully seal the lid and base together. Lay over the circle of greaseproof paper, followed by the pleated, double slayer of kitchen foil. Scrunch the foil around the pudding basin to seal. Lay the two lifting strips into a cross, place the pudding basin into the middle and lower into the slow cooker. Use a jug to carefully pour in enough hot water into the slow cooker so that it is about $^1/_3$ full. Cover with the slow cooker lid and cook on low for 7-8 hrs.

Once cooked, and protecting your hands from the heat, use the strips lifters to help you lift the pudding out of the slow cooker. Remove the foil and greaseproof paper on top. You can serve the pudding straight from the bowl, but it is much more impressive to slide a palette knife between the pudding and the bowl to loosen it and then and turn the whole thing out on to a serving plate.

Sweet Suet Pastry GF DF NF OF V Ve YF

Ingredients

- 180g (1¼ Cups) gluten-free Plain (All Purpose) Flour Blend
- 20g (2½ tbsp) Cornflour/Corn starch
- 90g (²/₃ Cup) gluten-free Vegetable Suet*
- 2 tsp gluten-free Baking Powder
- ½ tsp Xanthan Gum
- 2 tsp Vanilla Sugar
- 1 tsp Lemon Zest or 1 tsp Ground Cinnamon or Seeds from 1 Vanilla Pod

Directions

In a large bowl, whisk together all the dry ingredients (including the ground cinnamon, if using). Add the suet (and the finely grated lemon zest, if using) and use a table knife to mix it in until all the ingredients are well blended. Measure 120ml (½ Cup) of cold water into a jug (and add the seeds from the Vanilla Pod, if using).

Start to bring the pastry together by adding a tbsp of cold water and mixing to combine with the knife. Keep adding a little more water at a time until the pastry comes together into a soft dough. Don't worry about using only part of the water and having quite a lot left over. Precisely how much water you need depends on a number of different factors which Makes: it hard to be exact on how much liquid you'll need. So, just take it slowly, don't add too much water in one go, and you will get to the stage when you have a ball of soft dough, with a few bits of flour/fat left over.

At this point, use clean hands to knead the dough fully together and leaving the sides of the bowl clean. Wrap the ball of dough in kitchen wrap and chill in the fridge for 20 mins.

Use this pastry to make steamed puddings such as my Steamed Toffee Apple Pudding.

Note: Suet is a shredded white fat, originally from animal although my recipes use the vegetarian version, which is lower in saturated fat. Although suet is readily available in the UK, the leading brand is not gluten-free. In North America, it is not widely available at all. UK Readers can find recommendations on gluten-free sources of Vegetarian Suet in the Resource chapter of this book. However, an alternative method to create a shredded fat, especially for North American Readers, is to freeze a block of vegetable fat/shortening, and then coarsely grate it to the required quantity. This may sound a lot of fuss, but suet pastry is so easy to make, even if you are someone that normally struggles with pastry, so it is worth the effort.

Makes: **enough to line a 1-1.2L (4-5 Cup) pudding basin**   Ready In: **30 mins** inc chilling time

Steamed Toffee Apple Pudding

Ingredients

- 1 quantity of Sweet Suet Pastry, flavoured with Vanilla Seeds, chilled
- 285g (10 oz) Cooking Apples such as Bramley (peeled and cored weight)
- 285g (10 oz) crisp Eating Apples such as Coxes or Fuji (peeled and cored weight)
- 100g (½ Cup, packed) Light Brown Sugar
- 55g (½ Stick) Butter + extra to grease the pudding basin
- 1½ tsp ground Cinnamon
- Pinch freshly grated Nutmeg
- Extra gluten-free Plain (All Purpose) Flour Blend to roll out the pastry

Directions

Peel, core and slice the apples. Place in a bowl, add the cinnamon, nutmeg and sugar and toss well. Grease a heat-proof 1L (4 Cup) pudding basin with butter. Cut a circle of baking parchment 2.5cm/1" wider than the top of the pudding basin. Prepare a piece of kitchen foil 50cm/20" long. Fold in half to create a double layer and then fold a 2.5cm/1" pleat into the centre.

Take your chilled dough and set aside about ¼ to use as a lid. Roll out the larger piece between two well-floured sheets of greaseproof paper into a circle shape large enough to line your pudding basin with a short overlap if about 2.5cm/1". The pastry will be quite "short" ie fragile. If you can transfer it from the sheet of greaseproof into the pudding basin in one go, then brilliant! If it breaks up, don't worry at all. Just patchwork together pieces of rolled pastry into the bowl to line it, pressing with your fingers to join the pieces together to make sure that there are no gaps and the basin is fully lined. Once you have lined the basin, roll out the retained pastry between flour-dusted greaseproof papers to a circle large enough to form a lid.

Spoon in the apple mixture, dotting with tsps of the butter as you go, so that the butter is evenly distributed throughout the filling. Dampen the basin pastry rim and carefully lift over the pastry lid. Press all around to fully seal the lid and base together. Lay over the circle of greaseproof paper, followed by the pleated, double slayer of kitchen foil. Scrunch the foil around the pudding basin to seal. Transfer to a steamer and steam for 3-4 hrs. Check occasionally to ensure that the steamer doesn't need topping up with water.

Once cooked, and protecting your hands from the heat, lift the pudding out of the steamer. Remove the foil and greaseproof paper on top. You can serve the pudding straight from the bowl, or slide a palette knife between the pudding and the bowl to loosen it and then turn out on to a serving plate. Serve piping hot with custard or cream.

Make this Dairy-Free/Vegan? Replace the butter with dairy-free margarine.

Serves: 6-8   Ready In: 4 hrs

SHORTCRUST PASTRY

Ingredients

- 175g (1¼ Cups) gluten-free Plain (All Purpose) Flour Blend
- 25g (4 tbsp) Cornflour/Corn starch
- 125g (1 Stick + 1 tbsp) Butter, very well chilled
- ¾ tsp gluten-free Baking Powder
- 1 tsp Xanthan Gum
- ¼ tsp Sea (Kosher) Salt
- 1 UK Large (US Extra Large) Free Range Egg, chilled
- 1-2 tbsp Milk, chilled

Directions

Sift the flour, cornflour/corn starch, baking powder, salt and xanthan gum into the bowl of a stand food mixer fitted with a paddle beater or into a food processor. Cut the butter into dice and add to the flour mix. Blend in the food mixer until the mixture resembles breadcrumbs.

In a small jug, whisk together the egg and milk. Initially, add ¾ of the wet mixture to the dry mixture and pulse the mixer until the dough comes together into a sticky dough. Add a little more of the wet mix of the dough is too dry. If necessary, use your (clean) hands to finally knead the dough together. Retain any left over wet mix (covering the jug with kitchen film) to use as an egg wash on the pastry before baking.

Wrap the ball of dough in kitchen wrap, pat it down and chill in the fridge for 20 mins.

Use this pastry to make savoury or sweet pies or tarts, such as my Family Chicken, Leek and Mushroom Pie.

Make this Dairy-Free? Replace the butter with well-chilled dairy-free margarine and the semi-skimmed milk with dairy-free milk.

Makes: **enough to top a 20cm/8" pie dish** Ready In: **30 mins** inc chilling time

Family Chicken, Leek & Mushroom Pie GF NF OF YF

Ingredients

- 1 quantity of Shortcrust Pastry, chilled
- Extra gluten-free Plain (All Purpose) Flour Blend to roll out the pastry
- 250g (2½ Cups) Fennel, chopped
- 2 medium Leeks, trimmed
- 240g (2 Cups) Mushrooms
- 240ml (1 Cup) White Wine
- 240ml (1 Cup) Milk

- 120ml (½ Cup) Crème Fresh
- 4 tbsp Cornflour/Corn starch
- 700g (1½ lb) Chicken Breasts
- ½ tsp freshly ground Black Pepper
- ¼ tsp Sea (Kosher) Salt
- 2 tsp dried Herbs de Provence
- 2 tsp of Olive Oil

Directions

Slice the leeks, rinse them and drain thoroughly. Dice the fennel and slice the mushrooms. Heat 1 tsp of olive oil in a sauté pan over a medium heat and add the leeks and fennel. Cook for 5 mins. Add the mushrooms and continue to sauté until golden. Transfer to a plate/bowl whilst you cook the chicken. Cut the chicken into bite size pieces.

Heat the remaining 1 tsp of olive oil in the sauté pan over a medium heat and cook the chicken pieces in batches, until golden. Transfer cooked batches to the same bowl as the sautéed vegetables. Once all the chicken is cooked, return the chicken/vegetables to the sauté pan and pour over the white wine. Season with salt, pepper and add the dried herbs. Bring up to the simmer and simmer on a low heat for 10 mins.

Dissolve the cornflour/corn starch in the milk and whisk into the sauté pan. Keep stirring in the pan until the sauce thickens. Remove from the heat and set to one side.

Preheat the oven to 170C fan, 375F, Gas Mark 5.

Take your chilled dough and roll out between two well-floured sheets of greaseproof paper into a shape slightly larger than your pie dish. Stir the Crème Fresh into the chicken mixture and pour it into the pie dish. Still in the greaseproof paper, flip the pastry over and remove the sheet that is now upmost. Use the remaining greaseproof paper to help you transfer the pastry over the pie dish. Trim the edges and crimp using two fingers and a thumb. If you are feeling artistic, re-roll any pastry trimmings and cut out 4 leaf shapes for decoration.

Brush the pie top using the retained spare egg/milk mix from making pastry, cut a small cross in the middle and decorate with the pastry leaf shapes. Brush these with egg wash too. Place onto a baking sheet and pop into the oven. Bake for 45 mins until the pie crust is golden brown and the filling is piping hot.

Serves: 6   Ready In: 1 hr 10 mins

SWEET SHORTCRUST PASTRY

Ingredients

- 175g (1¼ Cups) gluten-free Plain (All Purpose) Flour Blend
- 25g (4 tbsp) Cornflour/Corn starch
- 100g (7 tbsp) Butter, very well chilled
- 20g (1¾ tbsp) solid white Vegetable Fat eg Trex (UK), Crisco (US) very well chilled
- ¾ tsp gluten-free Baking Powder
- 1 tsp Xanthan Gum
- 4 tsp Vanilla Sugar (or Natural Caster (Superfine) Sugar)
- $^1/_8$ tsp Sea (Kosher) Salt
- 1 UK Large (US Extra Large) Free Range Egg, chilled
- 1-2 tbsp Milk, chilled
- 1 Vanilla Pod (optional)*

Note: The vanilla seeds add a depth of flavour to this sweet pastry and vanilla is a flavouring used in many sweet pie or tart recipes. However, if the dish you need the pastry for will not be enhanced with this hint of vanilla, then just leave it out.

Directions

Sift the flour, cornflour/corn starch, baking powder, sugar, salt and xanthan gum into the bowl of a stand food mixer fitted with a paddle beater or into a food processor. Cut the butter and vegetable fat into dice and add to the flour mix. Blend in the food mixer until the mixture resembles breadcrumbs.

In a small jug, whisk together the egg and milk. Initially, add ¾ of the wet mixture to the dry mixture. Scrape the seeds from the vanilla pod (if using) and add these to the bowl. Now pulse the mixer until the dough comes together into a sticky dough. Add a little more of the wet mix of the dough is too dry. If necessary, use your (clean) hands to finally knead the dough together. Retain any left over wet mix (covering the jug with kitchen film) to use as an egg wash on the pastry before baking.

Wrap the ball of dough in kitchen wrap, pat it down and chill in the fridge for 20 mins.

Use this pastry to make sweet pies or tarts, such as my Bakewell Tarts.

Make this Dairy-Free? Replace the butter with well-chilled dairy-free margarine and the semi-skimmed milk with dairy-free milk.

Makes: **enough to top a 20cm/8" pie dish** Ready In: **30 mins** inc chilling time

Bakewell Tarts

Ingredients

- ½ quantity of Sweet Shortcrust Pastry, chilled*
- 60g (½ Stick) room temperature Butter, plus extra for greasing
- 60g (4 tbsp) Caster (Superfine) Sugar
- 60g (½ Cup) Ground Almonds
- 1 UK Medium (US Large) Free Range Egg, chilled
- ½ tsp Vanilla Extract
- 1 ½ tbsp Raspberry Jam
- 25g (¹/₃ Cup) Flaked Almonds
- 4 tbsp Icing (Confectioners) Sugar
- Extra gluten-free Plain (All Purpose) Flour Blend to roll out the pastry

Note: The left-over ½ quantity of sweet shortcrust pastry can be placed into a freezer bag and frozen. Also, the tarts can be frozen before their final baking. Do this by blind freezing in the bun tin, then once frozen, remove from the tin to a freezer bag. You can then bake off tarts as you want them.

Directions

Grease a 12-hole bun, cut 12 circles of baking parchment to fit . Preheat the oven to 180C fan, 400F, Gas Mark 6.

Take your chilled dough and roll out between two well-floured sheets of greaseproof paper to a thickness of 3mm. Cut out 12 rounds using an 8cm/3 ½" fluted cutter, re-rolling your pastry if necessary to get to 12 rounds. Use a palette knife to transfer each round to the bun tin and press into the hole. When all 12 are completed, prick the bases with a fork and pop the tin into the fridge to chill for 10 mins.

Line each pastry case with one circle of parchment and fill with baking beans or dried beans. Blind bake for 10 mins, until just turning golden and firm to touch. Remove the parchment and beans, then bake for further 3 mins until golden and crisp. Remove from the oven and turn the temperature down to 160C fan, 350F, Gas Mark 4.

Meanwhile, in a food mixer, beat together the butter, sugar, egg, ground almonds and vanilla extract. Put ½ tsp of jam in each tart case and then divide the frangipane paste evenly between the tarts. Smooth out the frangipane paste with a knife and then scatter over the flaked almonds.

Bake for 18-20 mins, or until the frangipane is just set and golden. Remove from the oven, allow to cool for 10 mins then transfer to a cooling rack.

In a small bowl, mix the icing sugar with a little water to make a runny icing. Drizzle the icing over the tarts in a zigzag pattern and leave to set. The tarts can be served warm or at room temperature.

Make this Dairy-Free? Replace the butter with dairy-free margarine.

Makes: 12   Ready In: 1 hr

Breads, Pizzas, & Batters

Crusty French Boule

Ingredients

- 1 tsp Olive Oil
- 1 tbsp Sunflower Oil
- ½ tsp Sea (Kosher) Salt
- ½ tbsp Sugar
- 5g (1½ tsp) Fast Action Dried Yeast
- 1 UK Large (US Extra Large) Free Range Egg
- 225g (1½ Cups) Gluten-Free Bread Flour Blend
- Optional - 1½ tsp Xanthan Gum (only required if using a Bread Flour Blend that doesn't include this)

Directions

In the bowl of a food mixer, whisk together the flour, sugar, yeast and salt. In a jug, whisk together the oils and 160ml (²/₃ Cup) lukewarm water. Make a well in the centre of the flour blend and break in the egg. Pour on ¹/₃ of the oil/water, mix together on low. Whisk the oil/water again and pour on another third, mix again on low. Finally add the last third of liquid and thoroughly beat together to dough. Lightly oil a round-bottomed bowl and transfer in the dough. Cover with kitchen film and leave to prove somewhere warm and draft-free for 2 hrs.

After 2 hrs, tip the dough onto a large oblong of parchment paper on a chopping board. If you've used a round-bottomed bowl, your dough should already have a nice, rounded Boule shape. Wet clean hands with water and lightly stroke the dough to smooth out the surface of the Boule. Bring up the parchment then cover again with kitchen film. Prove somewhere warm and draft-free for a further 75 mins to 90 mins.

Twenty mins before baking, preheat the oven to 240C fan, 500F, Gas Mark 10 and also preheat a lidded cast-iron Le Creuset/Dutch Oven (suitable for use at this temperature). When ready to bake, remove the kitchen film, then use a serrated knife to cut 3-4 slashes across the top of the Boule (clean the knife between cuts). Protecting your hands from the heat, take out the cast iron pan, place the dough still on the parchment paper into the pan and replace the lid. Return to the oven and bake for 20 mins, then remove the lid and turn the oven down to 210C fan, 450F, Gas Mark 8 for a further 15 mins. After that, take out of the oven and leave to cool in the pot.

Serves: 8-12   Ready In: 4 ½ hrs   inc proving time

Welsh Rarebit

Ingredients

- 3 UK Large (US Extra Large) Free Range Eggs
- 1 tbsp Cornflour/Corn starch
- 120ml (½ Cup) Milk
- ½ tsp gluten-free Dry Mustard Powder
- 40g ($^1/_3$ Cup) coarsely grated Mature Cheddar
- 35g ($^1/_3$ Cup) finely grated Parmesan
- 2 tsp gluten-free Worcestershire Sauce*
- Pinch freshly grated Nutmeg
- Pinch freshly ground Black Pepper
- 8 slices gluten-free French Boule or other Gluten-Free Bread

Note: In the UK, the leading brand of Worcestershire Sauce is not gluten-free, although the same brand in the US is gluten-free. UK readers can find recommendations on gluten-free sources of Worcestershire Sauce in the Resource chapter at the end of this book.

Directions

In a small jug, dissolve the cornflour/corn starch in 2 tbsp of the milk, and pour the remainder of the milk into a small saucepan. Heat over a medium heat until scalding. Whisk the cornflour/corn starch slurry again to make sure that it is fully slackened then whisking all the time, pour over the hot milk. Return the combined mixture to the saucepan and simmer for 1-2 mins until the sauce has thickened. Whisk in the mustard powder, Worcestershire sauce, nutmeg and black pepper, followed by the grated cheeses. Remove from the heat and whisk until the cheeses have melted into the sauce.

Separate the egg whites into a mixing bowl then add the egg yolks, one at a time, into the cheese sauce, beating well to combine after each addition.

Preheat the grill/broiler to medium heat.

Put the bread onto toast. Meanwhile, whisk the egg whites until stiff. Slacken the cheese sauce by stirring in 1 large spoonful of beaten egg white then carefully fold-in the remainder. Spread the toasts out onto a baking sheet or grill pan and spoon the Welsh Rarebit mixture onto each slice. Place the Rarebits under the grill/broiler and grill until they turn puffy and golden brown, serve immediately.

Serves: 4   Ready In: **30 mins**

CHOCOLATE CHIP BRIOCHE

GF NF OF V

Ingredients

- 100g (7 tbsp) Butter, very well chilled
- ½ tsp Sea (Kosher) Salt
- 1 tsp Vanilla Extract
- 4.5g (1⅓ tsp) Fast Action Dried Yeast
- 35g (3 tbsp) Gluten-Free Dark Chocolate Chips
- 2 UK Medium (US Large) Free Range Eggs
- 2 tbsp (28g) Natural Caster (Superfine) Sugar
- Rounded ½ tsp Xanthan Gum
- ¼ Cup + 1 tbsp (75ml) Semi-Skimmed Milk, divided
- 235g (1⅔ Cups) Gluten-Free Plain (All Purpose) Flour Blend

Directions

Pop the chocolate chips into a small ramekin. Place a sieve over the mixing bowl of a stand mixer and weigh out the flour. Remove ¼ tsp of flour and add to the chocolate chips, tossing them so that they are coated. Set aside until later. Add the xanthan gum to the flour and sift together. Add the salt and yeast and give the dry ingredients a quick mix to blend together with the k-paddle blade of the food mixer. Dice the chilled butter into cubes and add to the flour mix. Blend until the mixture resembles fine breadcrumbs. Add the sugar and mix again to combine.

Change the attachment on your stand mixer from the paddle blade to the balloon whisk attachment. Make a well in the centre. Measure ¼ cup + 1 tsp (65ml) of the milk into a jug and pour into the flour well. Break the eggs into the jug and whisk lightly, then pour all but 1 tsp into the well. Add the reserved 2 tsp of milk to the small amount of remaining egg in the jug, then whisk together then store in the fridge until later. Whisk together the wet and fry ingredients on a medium speed for 10 mins (the dough is more of a paste, not a conventional bread dough). Then cover with a clean kitchen towel and leave to rise for 1 hour.

Line a 12-hole muffin tin with paper cases or baking parchment. Stir the chocolate chips into the risen dough until well combined. Spoon the dough evenly into the bun tin. Cover loosely with the same clean kitchen towel and leave to prove for 3 hrs until light, puffy and doubled in size. Preheat the oven to 180C fan, 350F, Gas Mark 6. Use a pastry brush to brush the retained egg/milk mixture over the top on the buns. Bake for 20 minutes until golden brown. Leave to cool for 2–3 mins, then transfer to a wire rack to cool.

Make this Dairy-Free? Replace the butter with well-chilled dairy-free margarine and the semi-skimmed milk with dairy-free milk.

Makes: 6 large or 12 small   Ready In: 4 hrs 40 mins inc proving time

CORN TORTILLAS (GF) (DF) (NF) (OF) (V) (Ve) (YF)

Ingredients

- 65g/5½ oz Masa Harina Flour*
- 2 tsp Olive Oil, divided
- pinch Sea (Kosher) Salt

Note: Masa Harina Flour is speciality Mexican flour made from cooked corn kernels that are soaked in lime before being ground into flour. Whilst not standard fare in most supermarkets, it is widely available online (see the chapter Resources – Gluten-Free Ingredients for some suggested sources).

Directions

In a large bowl, whisk together the flour and salt in a bowl. Measure out 45ml (3 tbsp) of cold water. Add 1 tsp olive oil to the bowl and enough water to mix into a smooth dough. Add a drop more water if the dough is too dry or a little more flour if it's too sticky. Divide the dough into 8 and hand-roll into balls. Cover with kitchen film and leave to rest in the fridge for 10 mins.

Press out the balls of dough into discs about 3mm / ⅛" thick. If you have a tortilla press to do this, great, but if not, use either your (clean!) hands or a rolling pin.

Heat ¼ tsp of olive oil in a griddle or frying over a medium heat. Cook the tortillas in batches (adding more oil as required), cooking for 1 min on each side or until lightly coloured.

Use for wraps or for Mexican dishes, such as my Chicken & Pepper Enchiladas.

Makes: 8   Ready In: 1 hr

Chicken & Pepper Enchiladas GF NF OF YF

Ingredients

- 8 Gluten-Free Corn Tortillas
- 500g Cooked Chicken
- 2 Red or Orange Bell Peppers
- 175g (¾ Cup) canned Pinto Beans
- 2-3 Red or Green Chillies
- 2 Garlic Cloves
- Bunch of fresh Coriander/Cilantro
- 1 Lime, divided
- 720ml (3 cups) Passata
- 2 tbsp Tomato Purée
- 170g (1½ Cups) grated Mature Cheddar Cheese

- 2 tsp Ground Coriander
- 2 tsp Ground Cumin
- 1½ tsp Chilli Powder
- 1½ tsp dried Oregano
- 2-3 dashes Tabasco Sauce
- ¼ tsp freshly ground Black Pepper
- ¼ tsp Sea (Kosher) Salt
- 2 tsp Sugar
- 120ml (½ Cup) Sour Cream
- 2 tsp Olive Oil

Serves: 4   Ready In: 1 hr

Directions

Deseed the peppers and cut the flesh into strips. Heat a non-stick sauté pan over a medium heat and add 1 tsp of olive oil. Sauté the pepper until lightly charred but still crisp (about 8 mins).

Meanwhile, peel the onions and finely dice. Deseed the chillies and finely mince along with the garlic. Remove the leaves from the fresh coriander/cilantro and finely mince the stalks.

When the pepper strips are cooked, transfer to a mixing bowl. Add a further tsp of olive oil to the sauté pan and add the onions. Cook over a medium heat until softened. Whilst the onions are sautéing, shred the chicken and add this to cooked pepper strips along with the rinsed, drained pinto beans and coriander/cilantro leaves. When the onions are softened and golden, add the minced chillies, garlic and coriander/cilantro stalks. Cook for a further minute, then add the spices and oregano. Stir through to warm them, then pour in the passata. Add the tomato purée, sugar, salt, pepper and 2-3 dashes of Tabasco (to taste). Cut the lime in half and squeeze in the juice from one ½ (keep the other half for later). Give the sauce a good stir to combine and simmer the sauce for 10 mins to thicken.

Preheat the oven to 170C fan, 375F, Gas Mark 5.

When the sauce is cooked, spoon about a quarter over the chicken/bean mix and toss well to combine. Grease a baking dish large enough to hold 8 enchiladas and spread 4 tbsps of enchilada sauce over the bottom. Take a corn tortilla and spoon in 1/8 of the filling. Roll up the tortilla and tuck into the baking dish. Repeat with the remaining tortillas. Spread the remaining enchiladas sauce over the top of tortillas and scatter over the grated cheese. Bake in the oven for 25-30 mins until golden and bubbling. Divide the sour cream into 8 ramekins and cut the retained lime half into 8 wedges. Once cooked, serve 2 enchiladas per person with a ramekin of sour cream and a lime wedge on the side.

Make this Dairy-Free? – Use dairy-free cheese in place of cheddar and dairy-free cream alternative with a squeeze of lemon juice in place of sour cream.

Make this Vegetarian? – Replace the chicken with mushrooms, and sauté these at the same time as the pepper strips.

Pizza Dough GF DF NF OF V

Ingredients

- 400g (2¾ Cups) Gluten-Free White Bread Flour Blend, plus extra for rolling
- 1 tsp Xanthan Gum (only required if not already included in the Bread Flour Blend,)
- 2½ tsp Sugar
- ½ tsp Sea (Kosher) Salt
- 7g (2 tsp) Fast Action Dried Yeast (1 sachet)
- ½ tsp Bicarbonate of Soda (Baking Soda)
- 2 tsp White Wine Vinegar
- 3 tbsp Olive Oil, plus extra to grease bowl
- 240ml (1 Cup) Milk
- 1 UK Large (US Extra Large) Free Range Egg

Directions

Activate the yeast by warming half the milk (in a saucepan or in a jug in the microwave) until it is lukewarm, then sprinkle over the dried yeast and sugar. Whisk together and set aside for 10 mins to get frothy.

Meanwhile in the bowl of a stand mixer, combine the flour blend, xanthan gum (if using) and salt. Give it a quick whisk to combine then make a well in the centre. In a ramekin, whisk together the vinegar and bicarbonate of soda (baking soda). Pour this into the well, followed by the egg, olive oil, the milky yeast mixture and about ¾ of the remaining milk. Turn the mixer onto low and beat together to form a smooth dough. Add more milk if the dough is too dry or a little more flour if it's too sticky. Transfer the dough into a lightly oiled bowl, cover with kitchen film and leave to prove in a warm place for 1 hr, until it has doubled in size.

Preheat the oven to 220C fan, 475F, Gas Mark 9 and put in a pizza stone or large baking sheet to warm.

Tip the proved dough onto a floured surface and divide into 4 equal pieces. One at a time, roll each quarter into a 30cm/12" circle. Taking care to protect your hands, remove the hot pizza stone/baking sheet from the oven and transfer over the rolled pizza base. Cover with the toppings of your choice (such as my Mediterranean Pizza) and return to the hot oven to cook for 10-12 mins, until golden brown and crispy.

Makes: 4   Ready In: 1 hr

Mediterranean Pizzas   OF

Ingredients

- 1 quantity of Pizza Base dough
- 480ml (4 Cups) Passata
- 2 tbsp Tomato Purée
- 1 Red Onion
- 1 Celery Stalk
- 1 tbsp fresh Parsley
- 1 tbsp fresh Basil
- 1 tsp dried Oregano
- ½ tsp Red Chili Flakes
- 2 Bay Leaves
- 240g (2 Cups) Chestnut Mushrooms

- 2 Garlic Cloves
- 2 tsp Olive Oil
- 2 tsp Sugar
- 1 tsp Sea (Kosher) Salt
- ½ tsp freshly ground Black Pepper
- 300g (2½ Cups) Mozzarella Cheese, grated
- 115g (1 Cup) Cheddar Cheese, grated
- 50g (½ Cup) Parmesan Cheese, finely grated
- 12 canned Artichoke Hearts, rinsed and drained
- 6 slices Parma Ham

Directions

Whilst the pizza dough is proving, prepare the toppings and make the Marinara Sauce. Clean the mushrooms and slice. Heat 1 tsp of olive oil in a sauté pan over a medium heat and add the mushrooms. Sauté until golden brown, then tip onto a plate and set aside. Peel the red onion and de-thread the celery (see my website post on why de-threading celery is a good idea) and finely dice along with the red onion. Heat another 1 tsp of olive oil in a sauté pan over a medium heat and add the diced vegetables. Sauté until softened. Finely mince the garlic and add to the pan, cook for a further minute. Finely chop the fresh parsley and basil then add these to the pan along with the dried herbs and seasonings. Pour in the passata and tomato purée along with the sugar. Give everything a good stir and leave to simmer gently for 15 mins until thickened. Set aside. Now grate the three types of cheese, cut the olives in halves and the artichokes into quarters.

Preheat the oven to 220C fan, 475F, Gas Mark 9 and put in a pizza stone or large baking sheet to warm.

Tip the proved dough onto a floured surface and divide into 4 equal pieces. One at a time, roll each quarter into a 30cm/12" circle. Taking care to protect your hands, remove the hot pizza stone/baking sheet from the oven and transfer over the rolled pizza base. Spread the base with a quarter of the sauce, top with a quarter of each of the toppings, roughly tearing the Parma ham by hand, then sprinkle with a quarter of each of the three cheeses. Return to the hot oven to cook for 10-12 mins, until golden brown and crispy.

Makes: 4   Ready In: 1 hr

Spiced Seeded Flatbreads GF NF OF V YF

Ingredients

- 400g (2 ¾ Cups) Gluten-Free White Bread Flour Blend, plus extra for rolling
- 1 tsp Xanthan Gum (only required if not already included in the Bread Flour Blend)
- ½ tsp Sea (Kosher) Salt
- 4 tsp gluten-free Baking Powder
- 300ml (1¼ Cups) Greek Yogurt
- 1 tbsp Olive Oil

- 2 tsp Cumin seeds
- 2 tsp Coriander seeds
- ¾ tsp Chilli Pepper Flakes
- 1 tbsp Pumpkin Seeds
- 1 tbsp Sunflower Seeds
- 1 tsp ground Cumin
- 1 tsp ground Coriander

Directions

Pre-heat a grill/broiler to a medium heat. Lightly dust a baking sheet with flour.

In a pestle and mortar, lightly crush the cumin and coriander seeds along with the chilli flakes (if you don't have a pestle and mortar, then use the end of a rolling pin and small bowl to crush the spices).

In a large bowl, whisk together the flour, xanthan gum, baking powder, spices, seeds and salt, then make a well in the centre. Stir in the Greek yogurt and olive oil along with 3 tbsp cold water. Mix together to form a soft dough, adding a little more water if the dough is too dry.

Turn onto a lightly floured surface and divide into 8 equal pieces. Shape into circles and roll each piece to a thin round about ½cm (¼") thick. Lightly dust with flour.

Grill/broil on the baking sheet for 3-5 mins on each side until golden and puffed. Serve warm with curries or chillies such as my Quick Prawn & Spinach Dahl.

Cooking for 1 or 2? Prepare & Freeze Tip:

Once cooked and cooled, flatbreads can be individually wrapped in kitchen foil and frozen. Once defrosted, reheat in the oven at 160C fan, 350F, Gas Mark 4 for about 3-5 minutes.

Note: These flatbreads are a wonderful accompaniment to warm winter soups as well as an alternative to serving rice with curries or chillies.

Makes: 8   Ready In: 20 Mins

Quick Prawn & Spinach Dahl GF DF NF OF YF

Ingredients

- 340g (12oz) Raw Shrimp/King Prawns
- 100g (½ Cup) Red Lentils, dry weight, rinsed
- 4 Medium Tomatoes
- 8 Cups (240g) Baby Spinach
- 2 Red Onions
- 1 Red Bell Pepper
- 1 tbsp freshly grated Ginger
- 2 Garlic Clove
- 8 Spiced Seeded Flatbreads

- 2 Red Chilli
- 2 tbsp gluten-free Medium Strength Curry Paste
- 1²/₃ Cup (400ml) Coconut Milk
- 1 bunch fresh Coriander/Cilantro
- 1 Lime
- 2 tsp Olive Oil
- Pinch Ground Black Pepper
- Pinch Sea (Kosher) Salt

Directions

Cut the red onions in half from top to bottom and finely slice. Remove the seeds and pith from the red pepper and red chillies. Cut the pepper into thick slices. Finely mince the red chillies along with the garlic clove. Peel the ginger and grate. Pick the leaves from the fresh coriander/cilantro and set aside for later. Finely mince the stalks.

Heat 2 tsp of olive oil in a lidded sauté pan or Dutch Oven over a medium heat. Add the onion and red pepper slices and cook for 5 minutes until softened and golden. Meanwhile, remove the skins from the tomatoes by placing them in a heat proof bowl and covering with boiling water for 1 min. Carefully remove from the water with a slotted spoon, and when cool enough to handle, slip off the skins and discard, then roughly chop the tomatoes.

Add the minced garlic, chilli, grated ginger and coriander/cilantro stalks to the pan. Cook for a further minute. Then stir in the curry paste and stir around the pan to release the fragrance of the spices. Add the coconut milk, rinsed red lentils and tomatoes, give everything a good stir, then cover and simmer gently for 20 mins. Stir the spinach and prawns into the curry and cook for a further 2-3 mins until the prawns are pink and cooked through and the spinach has wilted. Ladle into warm bowls, sprinkle with freshly chopped coriander and squeeze over the juice of a lime. Serve with the flatbreads on the side.

Serves: 4   Ready In: 30 mins

Yorkshire Puddings/
Pop-overs GF NF OF V YF

Ingredients

- 70g (½ Cup) Gluten-Free White Flour Blend
- 15g (2 tbsp) Cornflour (Corn starch)
- 1½ tsp gluten-free Baking Powder
- ½ tsp Xanthan Gum
- ¼ tsp Sea (Kosher) Salt
- 2 UK Large (US Extra Large) Free Range Eggs
- 240ml (1 Cup) Milk, chilled
- 30g (2 tbsp) Butter, melted
- 15g (1 tbsp) Vegetable Fat

Directions

Melt the butter in ramekin on low in the microwave or in a small saucepan. Set aside to cool. In a bowl, whisk together the flour, cornflour/corn starch, baking powder, xanthan gum and salt. Make a well in the centre, break in the eggs and pour over the cooled, melted butter. Using a handheld food mixer, start to whisk the eggs/butter into the flour. When this batter becomes thick (which will be before you have incorporated all the flour) start to add the milk, keeping whisking. Continue to whisk until all the milk in combined and you have a light, frothy batter. Transfer the batter to a jug, cover with kitchen film and chill in the fridge for 15-20 mins.

Preheat the oven 200C, 425F, Gas Mark 7. Divide the vegetable fat between the cavities of a 12-hole muffin tin and put this into the oven to heat up until the fat is very hot.

Carefully remove the muffin tin from the oven and evenly pour the batter between the cavities. Bake in the oven for 20-25 mins until beautifully risen and golden brown. Serve for a family Sunday Lunch.

Makes: 12   Ready In: 45 Mins

Cakes, Cupcakes & Bakes

CHOCOLATE GANACHE CELEBRATION CAKE

Cake Ingredients

- 50g (¹/₃ Cup) Plain (All-Purpose) Gluten-Free Flour Blend
- 25g (2 tbsp + 2tsp) Chestnut Flour*
- 1½ tsp Gluten-Free Baking Powder
- 130g (½ Cup + 1½ tbsp) Natural Caster (Superfine) Sugar
- 115g (1 stick) Butter at room temperature, plus a little extra for greasing
- 150g (5¹/₃ oz) 70% Cocoa Chocolate
- 3 UK Large (US Extra Large) Free Range Eggs
- ½ tsp Gluten-Free Instant Coffee Granules/Powder
- 1 tsp Vanilla Extract
- ½ tsp Glycerine (culinary Glycerol)
- ¹/₃ tsp Xanthan Gum
- Pinch Sea (Kosher) Salt

Icing Ingredients

- 115g (4 oz) 70% Cocoa Chocolate
- 115ml (½ Cup) Double (Heavy) Cream
- Sugar Flowers

Serves: 6-8   Ready In: 1 hr

Note: If you are unable to source Chestnut Flour, just replace with gluten-free flour blend.

Directions

Preheat the oven to 160C fan, 350F, Gas Mark 4. Grease and line two 15cm/6" cake tins with baking parchment.

Break up the chocolate into heatproof bowl. Fill a saucepan with enough water so that you can rest the bowl over the pan without the bottom of the bowl touching the water. Bring the water up to a gentle simmer and then rest the bowl over the pan. Stirring occasionally, allow the chocolate to melt completely, then set aside to cool.

Meanwhile, add the butter and sugar to the mixing bowl of a stand or hand-held food mixer. Beat together really well, (this should take at least 5 mins and preferably 10 mins). Whilst the butter and sugar is beating, check the melted chocolate and remove from the saucepan to cool if fully melted. Dissolve the instant coffee in 2 tsp of boiling water and set this aside to cool too. In a bowl, whisk together the flour blend, chestnut flour, baking powder, xanthan gum and salt.

When the butter/sugar mix is a light pale yellow and very fluffy, beat in the vanilla extract, Glycerine and cooled dissolved coffee, then gradually beat in the eggs, one at a time, until well mixed. Add half the cooled, melted chocolate, beat to combine, then add the remainder and beat again.

Add the flour mixture and, on a very low speed, beat until combined. Divide the mixture between the two cake tins and bake in the oven for 25 until firm to the touch and a skewer inserted in the centre comes out clean. Remove from the oven, leave to cool completely in the tins then turn out from the tins and remove the baking parchment.

While the cakes are baking, make the chocolate ganache. Break up the chocolate into heatproof bowl and add the cream. As before, fill a saucepan with enough water so that you can rest the bowl over the pan without the bottom of the bowl touching the water. Bring the water up to a gentle simmer and then rest the bowl over the pan. Melt the chocolate, stirring occasionally (don't worry that the mixture will look grainy whilst it is melting). Once the chocolate is fully melted, beat the chocolate/cream mixture until smooth and glossy. Remove from the heat, allow to cool to room temperature, then place in the fridge to chill.

When the cakes have cooled and the ganache has chilled, transfer the ganache to the bowl of a food mixer fitted with the paddle beater. Beat the ganache until it is light, airy and a paler in colour. Set the bottom cake layer onto a plate with the base side up, then spread over slightly less than half the beaten ganache. Top with the remaining cake layer and then spread this with the remaining beaten ganache. If you want a really smooth finish, dip a palette knife in hot water, dry then run over the top of the ganache. Repeat as desired. Decorate with sugar flowers.

Make this Dairy-Free? – Use dairy-free spread in place of butter and dairy-free cream in place of the cream.

Make this Nut-Free? – Replace the chestnut flour with flour blend.

Walnut & Coffee Cake GF OF V YF

Cake Ingredients

- 185g (1¼ Cups) Plain (All-Purpose) Gluten-Free Flour Blend
- 38g (5 tbsp) Cornflour (Corn starch)
- 220g (1 Cup) Natural Caster (Superfine) Sugar
- 225g (2 sticks) Spreadable Butter, plus a little extra for greasing
- 3 UK Large (US Extra Large) Free Range Eggs
- Pinch Sea (Kosher) Salt

- 75g (¾ Cup) Walnut Halves
- 2 tbsp Sour Cream
- 2 tsp gluten-free Instant Coffee Granules/Powder
- ¾ tsp Glycerine (culinary Glycerol)
- 3 tsp Gluten-Free Baking Powder
- ¾ tsp Bicarbonate of Soda (Baking Soda)
- ¾ tsp Xanthan Gum

Icing/Filling Ingredients

- 1 tsp gluten-free Instant Coffee Granules/Powder
- ½ tsp Vanilla Extract
- 50g Butter, at room temperature

- 115g Icing (Confectioners) Sugar
- 12 Walnut Halves

Directions

Preheat the oven to 160C fan, 350F, Gas Mark 4. Grease and line two 20cm/8" cake tins with baking parchment. Dissolve the coffee in 2 tsp boiling water, set aside. Finely chop the walnut halves. Cream together the butter and sugar in the mixing bowl of a stand or hand-held food mixer, beating for at least 5 mins. Meanwhile, in a separate bowl, whisk together the flour blend, cornflour/corn starch, baking powder, baking soda, xanthan gum and salt. When the butter/sugar mix is pale yellow and very fluffy, add the coffee and glycerine, then gradually beat in the eggs, one at a time, until well mixed. On a low speed, beat in half the flour mix followed by the sour cream, then add the remaining flour and beat until to combined. Finally, add the chopped walnuts and mix again.

Divide the mixture between the two cake tins and bake in the oven for 25 until firm to the touch and a skewer inserted in the centre comes out clean. Remove from the oven, leave to cool completely in the tins then turn out and remove the lining. Meanwhile, dissolve the coffee for the frosting in 2 tsp of hot water and leave to cool. Beat the butter in a clean bowl. Turn off the mixer and add half the icing sugar. Turn the mixer back on the lowest setting and beat the butter and icing sugar together. Add the cooled coffee and vanilla extract and beat to mix. Turn off the mixer, add the remaining sugar, turn back on lowest setting and beat to combine. Once all the sugar is combined, turn the mixer up to the highest speed and beat the buttercream for 5 mins until it is light and mousse-like. Set the bottom cake layer onto a plate with the base side up, then spread over half the buttercream. Top with the remaining cake layer and then spread this with the remaining buttercream. Decorate with the walnut halves.

Make this Dairy-Free? – Use dairy-free spread in place of butter and dairy-free cream in place of the sour cream.

Serves: 8-12   Ready In: 1 hr

Dairy-Free Walnut & Banana Tea Loaf GF DF OF V YF

Cake Ingredients

- 175g (1 Cup plus 3 tbsp) Plain (All-Purpose) Gluten-Free Flour Blend
- 25g (3 tbsp) Chestnut Flour
- 25g (4 tbsp) Cornflour (Corn starch)
- 2 tsp Gluten-Free Baking Powder
- ½ tsp Xanthan Gum
- 2 tbsp Demerara (Turbinado) Sugar
- 110g (½ Cup, packed, + 1 tbsp) Light Brown Sugar

- 80g (²/₃ stick) Sunflower Spread
- 1 UK Large (US Extra Large) Free Range Egg
- 4 medium, ripe Bananas
- 60g (²/₃ Cup) Walnut Halves
- 1 Orange
- 1½ tsp ground Cinnamon
- Pinch Sea (Kosher) Salt

Note: If you are unable to source Chestnut Flour, just replace with gluten-free flour blend.

Directions

Preheat the oven to 160C fan, 350F, Gas Mark 4. Line a 0.9L (2 lb) Loaf Tin with a paper loaf tin liner.

Roughly chop the walnut halves, place in a small bowl along with the finely grated zest from the orange. Toss in 2 tsps of flour (taken from the measured amount of flour for the recipe).

In the mixing bowl of a stand or hand-held food mixer, whisk together the flours, salt, cinnamon, baking powder, xanthan gum and light brown sugar. Add the sunflower spread and egg and beat together until fully combined (don't worry that at this stage it will still look at bit grainy).

Mash the bananas with a fork and add to the mixing bowl. Beat on low to combine. Finally, add the nuts and zest, and beat again on low until fully mixed. Pour into the loaf tin and smooth out with a spatula. Sprinkle over the Demerara (turbinado) sugar. Bake in the centre of the oven for 1hr 10min, until golden and a toothpick inserted in the centre comes out clean.

Remove from the oven and leave to cool in the tin for 20 mins, then transfer in the liner to a wire rack to cool completely.

Make this Dairy-Free? – Use dairy-free spread in place of butter.

Serves: 10   Ready In: 1½ hrs

Serves: 6-8   Ready In: 1 hr

Cake Ingredients

- 125g (1 Cup less 2 tbsp) Plain (All-Purpose) Gluten-Free Flour Blend
- 25g (4 tbsp) Cornflour (Corn starch)
- 150g ($^2/_3$ Cup) Natural Caster (Superfine) Sugar
- 150g ($1^1/_3$ sticks) Spreadable Butter, plus a little extra for greasing
- 2 UK Large (US Extra Large) Free Range Eggs
- 2 tbsp Sour Cream
- 1 Vanilla Pod
- ½ tsp Glycerine (culinary Glycerol)
- 2 tsp Gluten-Free Baking Powder
- ½ tsp Bicarbonate of Soda (Baking Soda)
- ½ tsp Xanthan Gum
- Pinch Sea (Kosher) Salt

Icing/Filling Ingredients

- 2 tbsp Raspberry Jam
- 120ml (½ Cup) Double (Heavy) Cream
- 2 tsp Icing (Confectioners) Sugar

Directions

Preheat the oven to 160C fan, 350F, Gas Mark 4. Grease and line two 15cm/6" cake tins with baking parchment.

Cream together the butter and sugar in the mixing bowl of a stand or hand-held food mixer, beating for at least 5 mins. Meanwhile, in a separate bowl, whisk together the flour blend, cornflour/corn starch, baking powder, baking soda, xanthan gum and salt. Split the vanilla pod and carefully scrape out the seeds. When the butter/sugar mix is a light pale yellow and very fluffy, add the seeds along with Glycerine, then gradually beat in the eggs, one at a time, until well mixed. Add half the flour mixture and, on a very low speed, beat until combined. Beat in the sour cream, then add the remaining flour and beat on low. Divide the mixture between the two cake tins and bake in the oven for 25 until firm to the touch and a skewer inserted in the centre comes out clean. Remove from the oven, leave to cool completely in the tins then turn out from the tins and remove the baking parchment.

When the cakes have cooled, whip the cream in a clean bowl until it forms soft peaks. Set the bottom cake layer onto a plate with the base side up, then spread over raspberry jam, followed by the whipped cream. Top with the remaining cake layer and then dust this with the icing sugar in a sieve.

Make this Dairy-Free? – Use dairy-free spread in place of butter and dairy-free cream in place of the cream.

PECAN CARROT TRAY BAKE

Cake Ingredients

- 200g (1¹/₃ Cup + 1 tbsp) Plain (All-Purpose) Gluten-Free Flour Blend
- 25g (4 tbsp) Cornflour (Corn starch)
- 190ml (¾ Cup + 2 tsp) Sunflower Oil
- 2 UK Large (US Extra Large) Free Range Eggs
- 150g (1¹/₃ Cups) coarsely grated Carrots
- 2 ½ tsp gluten-free Baking Powder
- 170g (¾ Cup, packed, + 5 tsp) Light Brown Sugar
- ½ tsp Bicarbonate of Soda (Baking Soda)
- ¾ tsp Glycerine (culinary Glycerol)
- ½ tsp Xanthan Gum
- 1 tsp ground Cinnamon
- 1 tsp ground Mixed Spice
- ½ tsp ground Ginger
- 1 tsp Vanilla Extract
- 60g (²/₃ Cup) Pecan Halves

Frosting Ingredients

- 75g (²/₃ stick) Butter, at room temperature
- 1 tsp Vanilla Extract
- 150g (²/₃ Cup) full-fat Cream Cheese, at room temperature
- 50g (7½ tbsp) Icing (Confectioners) Sugar
- 9 Pecan Halves

Directions

Preheat the oven to 160C fan, 350F, Gas Mark 4. Grease and line a 22cm/9" square cake tin.

Mix together the flour, cornflour/corn starch, baking powder, soda, xanthan gum and spices. Coarsely grate the carrots and chop the pecan nuts. In the bowl of a stand food mixer, beat together the sugar, oil, eggs, glycerine and vanilla extract until well combined, lighter and thicker. Add the grated carrots and chopped nuts and mix together. Add the flour mix and beat on a low speed until completely combined. Pour the mixture into the lined cake tin. Place in the oven and bake for about 35 mins or until golden brown, risen and firm to touch. Remove from the oven and leave to cool in the tin for 20 mins then transfer onto a wire rack, removing any baking parchment.

Meanwhile, in a clean bowl, beat together the butter, cream cheese and vanilla extract until well combined. Sift in the icing sugar, and beat again on low until smooth. Don't over beat the mixture. Spread the frosting over the cooled cake and decorate the top of the cake with the halved pecans, spaced evenly into the centre of 9 squares.

Make this Dairy-Free? – Use dairy-free spread and cream cheese in place of the butter and cream cheese.

Serves: 9   Ready In: 1 hr

Lemon & Blueberry Buttermilk Cupcakes GF NF OF V YF

Ingredients
- 110g (¾ Cup) Fresh or Thawed, Frozen Blueberries
- 15g (2 tbsp) Ground Almonds
- 140g (²/₃ Cup) Natural Caster (Superfine) Sugar
- 1½ tsp Gluten-Free Baking Powder
- ¹/₈ tsp Bicarbonate of Soda (Baking Soda)
- ½ tsp Xanthan Gum
- 55g (4 tbsp) Buttery Sunflower Spread
- 1 UK Large (US Extra Large) Free Range Egg
- 120ml (½ Cup) Buttermilk
- ¹/₈ tsp Sea (Kosher) Salt
- 120ml (½ Cup) Semi-Skimmed (2% Reduced-Fat) Milk
- 190g (1¹/₃ Cups) Plain (All-Purpose) Gluten-Free Flour Blend

Icing Ingredients
- 120g (1 Cup) Icing (Powdered) Sugar
- 1 Lemon, zest and juice, divided

Directions

Preheat the oven to 180C fan, 350F, Gas Mark 6. Line 2 muffin tins with 12 cupcake wrappers.

In a small saucepan, melt the buttery spread, and leave to cool slightly. In a jug, whisk together the egg, buttermilk, milk, the finely grated zest from the lemon and the melted spread. If using thawed frozen blueberries, thoroughly pat dry on kitchen paper. Set aside 12 to decorate the finished cakes then put the remainder in a small bowl and toss with 1 tbsp of flour (from the measured quantity of flour for the recipe).

In a stand or handheld food mixer, combine the flour, ground almonds, sugar, baking powder, soda, xanthan gum and salt. Make a well in centre of the dry mixture and pour in the buttermilk/egg mixture. Mix together on a low speed until well combined. Add the blueberries and mix again on low speed until combined. Spoon the batter into prepared cake wrappers. Bake for 15-20 minutes or until cupcakes spring back when touched lightly in centre. Remove from the oven and transfer to cool on wire racks.

Juice the lemon. Put the icing (powdered) sugar in jug and add enough lemon juice to slacken to thick, cream-like consistency. Use a teaspoon to spread over the cupcakes and decorate with the reserved blueberries.

Makes: 12   Ready In: 35 mins

CRANBERRY & ORANGE SCONES GF NF OF V YF

Ingredients

- 200g (1¹/₃ Cups + 1 tbsp) Gluten-Free Plain (All Purpose) Flour Blend, plus extra for rolling out
- 25g (4 tbsp) Cornflour (Corn starch)
- 2 tsp gluten-free Baking Powder
- ½ tsp Bicarbonate of Soda (Baking Soda)
- ½ tsp Xanthan Gum
- 1 tsp Glycerine (culinary Glycerol)
- ¹/₈ tsp Sea (Kosher) Salt

- 75g (5 tbsp) Butter, well chilled
- 50g (scant ½ Cup) Dried Cranberries
- 2 tsp fresh Orange Zest (from ½ Orange)
- 2 tbsp (25g) Natural Caster (Superfine) Sugar
- 1 tsp Vanilla Extract
- 1 UK Large (US Extra Large) Free Range Egg
- 2-3 tbsp Buttermilk

Makes: 7   Ready In: 1 hr

Directions

Preheat the oven to 180C, 375F, Gas Mark 6. Line a baking sheet with baking parchment.

In a large bowl, whisk together the flour blend, cornflour/corn starch, baking powder, bicarbonate of (baking) soda, xanthan gum and salt. Add the butter and use your fingertips to rub it into the flour until it resembles fine breadcrumbs. Stir the cranberries into the mixture along with the orange zest and sugar. Crack the egg into a small jug, add 2 tbsp buttermilk and vanilla extract, lightly whisk together. Make a bit of a well in the middle of the flour mixture with a round-bladed knife, then pour in most of this wet mixture, holding a little bit back in case it's not needed. Using the knife, gently work the mixture together until it forms a soft, almost sticky, dough. Work in any loose dry bits of mixture with the rest of the wet mixture.

Tip the dough onto a lightly floured work surface, knead briefly until smooth then roll it out to 4cm/1.5" thick. Using a 5.5cm (2.5") straight-sided pastry cutter, cut out 7 scones (don't twist as you cut), re-rolling the dough as you go.

Transfer the scones on the prepared baking sheet, making sure they are well spaced. Brush the tops with the extra buttermilk. Bake for 15 minutes until well risen and golden. Transfer to a cooling rack to cool.

Make this Dairy-Free? – Use dairy-free spread in place of butter.

Cooking for 1 or 2? Prepare & Freeze Tip:

Once the scones are cut out and brushed with the buttermilk, transfer to the freezer. You can then defrost and bake as many or as few scones as you need at a time. Gluten-free scones can stale more quickly, so if you want to keep the scones for a few days, it's better to freeze the raw scones and then cook them as and when you need them.

BANANA NUT BROWNIE BITES

GF OF V YF

Ingredients

- 28g (2 tbsp) Unsalted Butter, plus extra for greasing
- 60g (¼ Cup + 1 tsp) Natural Caster (Superfine) Sugar
- 1 US Large (UK Medium) Free Range Egg
- 50g (1¾ oz) 70%+ Cocoa Dark Chocolate
- 23g (2½ tbsp) Plain (All-Purpose) Gluten-Free Flour Blend
- 4g (½ tbsp) Cornflour/corn starch
- 11g (2 tbsp) Dutch Process Cocoa Powder
- 50g (3 tbsp) Mashed Banana
- ½ tsp Vanilla Extract
- ¼ Cup (30g) Walnut Pieces

Directions

Break the chocolate into small pieces and pop into a small, heat-proof bowl. Cube the butter and add to the bowl. Quarter fill a small saucepan with just boiled water and sit the bowl on top so it rests on the rim of the pan, not touching the water. Put the saucepan over a low heat until the butter and chocolate have melted, stirring occasionally to mix them, the remove the bowl from the pan. Alternatively, cover the bowl loosely with cling film and put in the microwave, for 30 sec blasts, until fully melted. Set aside to cool to room temperature. Roughly chop the walnut pieces. Sieve together the flour, corn starch and cocoa powder. Mash the banana. Preheat the oven to 160C fan, 350F, Gas Mark 4. Grease a mini muffin tin with butter or line it with mini paper cases.

With a handheld food mixer with beaters or stand mixer with a balloon whisk, beat together the sugar with egg until pale, thick and fluffy (this takes a good 5 mins). Pour in the cooled chocolate mix and vanilla extract and whisk again. Sieve in the flour/cocoa mix then, using a metal spoon or silicon spatula, gentle fold in the flour and cocoa by hand, taking care not to knock out the air out of the mixture. Finally, fold in the banana and walnuts. Divide the mixture evenly into the muffin tin. Give the tin a sharp rap on the worktop to remove any air bubbles, then pop into the oven and cook for 10-12 mins until the top has a shiny, papery crust. Remove from the oven and allow to fully cool in the tin. Run a knife around the brownies to loosen before turning out of the tin.

Make this Dairy-Free? – Use dairy-free spread in place of butter.

Make this Nut-Free? – Replace the walnuts with the same quantity of gluten-free chocolate chips.

Makes: 12   Ready In: 30mins

Vanilla Drops

Ingredients

- 45g (¹/₃ Cup) Plain (All-Purpose) Gluten-Free Flour Blend
- 5g (½ tbsp) Cornflour/corn starch
- 35g (2½ tbsp) Natural Caster (Superfine) Sugar
- 2 tbsp (30g) Butter, melted
- 1 UK Medium (US Large) Free Range Egg
- ½ tsp Gluten-Free Baking Powder
- ¹/₈ tsp Xanthan Gum
- 1 tsp Vanilla Extract
- ½ tsp Glycerine (culinary Glycerol)
- ½ Vanilla Pod

Directions

Preheat the oven to 180C fan, 400F, Gas Mark 6.
Line a baking sheet with non-stick parchment.

Place the butter in a small microwave-proof jug, cover, and then microwave on low in 10 sec blasts until the fat has melted. Set aside. Mix together the flour, corn starch, baking powder and xanthan gum. In a stand or handheld food mixer, beat together the sugar with egg until thick and fluffy. Split the ½ vanilla pod in half length wise, scrape out the seeds and add to the mixture along with the vanilla extract and melted butter. Sieve in the flour mix then gentle fold everything together with a large metal spoon, taking care not to knock out the air.

Use a teaspoon to spoon 12 small rounds of the mixture onto the sheet, making sure they are well spaced out. Bake for 8 minutes until set and golden. Leave to cool.

Make this Dairy-Free? – Replace the butter with buttery sunflower spread.

Makes: 12   Ready In: 25mins

Roasted Strawberries & Cream Cheesecake

Ingredients

- 1 Quantity of Vanilla Drop Recipe
- 300g (2 Cups) Strawberries
- 325g (1¹⁄₃ Cups) Cream Cheese
- 175g (¾ Cup) Sour Cream
- 2 US Large (UK Medium) Free Range Eggs
- 110g + 2 tbsp (½ Cup + 2 tbsp) Natural Caster (Superfine) Sugar
- 1 tsp Vanilla Extract
- ½ Vanilla Bean Pod

Directions

Preheat the oven to 180C fan, 400F, Gas Mark 6. Line a roasting dish with non-stick parchment. Grease the base and sides of a 18cm/7" spring-form cake, and line the base with baking parchment.

Set aside 3 strawberries for decoration and hull the rest. Put into the roasting dish and sprinkle with the 2 tbsp of sugar and toss. Roast in the oven for 35 mins then allow to cool.

Meanwhile make up the vanilla drop recipe according to the instructions, but instead of making individual drops, pour into the cake tin. Bake in the oven for 12-15 mins until set and golden. Leave to cool.

Once the base and strawberries are both cooked and cooled, make the cheesecake filling. Reheat the oven to 180C fan, 400F, Gas Mark 6. In a large bowl, beat together the cream cheese and remaining sugar. Add the sour cream and beat again, then beat in the eggs one at a time. Pour half the mixture into a large jug. Split the vanilla pod and scrape out the seeds. Add these to the mixture in the jug along with the vanilla extract, whisk to combine. Fold the roasted strawberries into the other mixture in the bowl,

Pour the strawberry cheesecake mix into the tin over the sponge base. Place the cake tin into a large roasting tin and pour 2" of boiling water around the cake tin to create a bain-marie. Finally, swirl the vanilla mix in the jug over the strawberry mixture, pouring the mix over the back of spoon as you do it.

Carefully transfer the roasting dish to the oven and bake for 30 mins or until the cheesecake is set but still with a bit of a wobble in the centre. Turn off the oven but leave the cheesecake in the oven until it has cooled. Keep in the tin and put in the fridge to chill.

When ready to serve, run a knife around the edge before undoing the spring-form side of the tin. If you don't feel confident transferring the cheesecake from the base, don't worry, just put it on a pretty serving plate leaving it on the base. Decorate with the reserved strawberries.

Serves: 6   Ready In: 1 hr 30 mins

Puddings & Desserts

Chocolate Raspberry Pavlova

Ingredients

- 4 US Large (UK Med) Free Range Egg Whites
- 195g (¾ Cup + 2 tbsp) Natural Caster (Superfine) Sugar
- 2 tbsp gluten-free Cocoa Powder (Dutch process)
- 2 tsp Cornflour/Corn starch
- 1 tsp White Wine Vinegar
- 240ml (1 Cup) Double (Heavy) Cream
- 35g (4 tbsp) Dark Chocolate, chopped, plus a little extra for decoration
- 200g (1½ Cups) Fresh Raspberries

Directions

Preheat the oven to 180C fan, 400F, Gas Mark 6. Draw a 18cm/7" circle onto the parchment (trace around a cake tin or plate). Turn the parchment over so that that the drawn side is underneath (but you should still be able to see the circle to use as a template) and line a baking sheet.

Add the egg whites to the (very clean!) bowl of a food mixer fitted with the balloon whisk attachment. Whisk the egg whites until they just form stiff peaks (don't over-whisk). Turn the mixer down to low and beat in the sugar a spoonful at a time until the meringue is stiff and shiny. Turn off the processor, and sift in the cornflour/corn starch and cocoa, and pour in the vinegar. Whisk on low until combined. Finely chop the chocolate and gently fold in. Spoon onto the baking sheet, using the drawn circle as a template, and smooth out to an even thickness.

Place in the oven, then immediately turn the temperature down to 150C fan, 300F, Gas Mark 2. Bake for 1hr then turn off the oven, open the door slightly, and leave to cool completely.

It's best to assemble the Pavlova just before serving. Whisk the cream until thick and soft. Carefully peel the baking parchment from the bottom of the Pavlova and place on a cake plate. Spread the cream on top, then scatter over the raspberries. Finally, coarsely grate over the reserved chocolate and serve.

Make this Dairy-Free? – Use dairy-free cream alternative instead of cream.

Serves: 4-6   Ready In: 1 hr 15 mins plus chilling time

ROASTED SPICED PINEAPPLE

Ingredients

- 1 Ready Prepared Pineapple c 450g / lb
- ¼ Cup + 2 tsp (65g) Natural Caster (Superfine) Sugar
- 4 Cardamom Pods
- 1 Vanilla Pod
- Pinch Saffron

- 1 Star Anise
- 1 Cinnamon Stick
- 1 Lime
- 4 Black Peppercorns

Directions

Preheat the oven to 180C, 375F, Gas Mark 6.

Zest the lime then juice it into a jug. Add enough cold water to bring it up to 100ml/ $^1/_3$ Cup + 1 tbsp water. Pour into a saucepan along with the lime zest and sugar. Split the vanilla pod and scrape out the seeds, add the seeds and the pod to the saucepan. Use the back of a teaspoon to crack open the cardamom pods and breaks the cinnamon stick into 3. Add all the spices to the saucepan.

Over a medium heat, bring the spice mixture to the boil, stirring well so that the sugar dissolves, then reduce the heat to a simmer and cook for 5-8 minutes until it has thickened to a syrup. Taking care with the hot syrup, strain into a heat-proof jug to remove the whole spices.

Cut the pineapple into 8 even-sized wedges. Cut away the core if it is really tough.

Take 4 pieces of parchment paper, each approx 12"x18"/ 30cmx45cm approx. Place 1 sheet onto a baking sheet and place 2 wedges of pineapple into the centre of the parchment. Pour over a quarter of the spiced syrup. Seal the papillote by bringing the parchment up over the pineapple and then double-folding along the long edge, then fold over the two shorter edges and tuck under the parcel. The parcel should not be too tight, as steam will puff it up in the oven, but the edges do need to be fully sealed to prevent steam/liquid escaping whilst cooking. Repeat for the remaining 3 parcels.

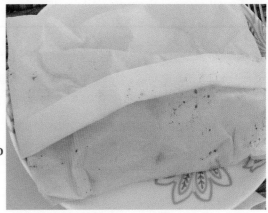

Place the baking sheet in the oven and cook for 10- 12mins. Remove from oven and allow to rest for 2 mins. Then to serve, place a papillote on a warm dessert plate and simply carefully pull open the papillote to eat.

Serves: 4   Ready In: 20 mins

STICKY DATE & PECAN PUDDINGS WITH BUTTERSCOTCH SAUCE

GF OF V YF

Pudding Ingredients

- 125g (1 Cup less 2 tbsp) Plain (All-Purpose) Gluten-Free Flour Blend
- 25g (4 tbsp) Chestnut Flour
- 25g (4 tbsp) Cornflour (Corn starch)
- 1½ tsp gluten-free Baking Powder
- ¼ tsp Xanthan Gum
- ¾ tsp Bicarbonate of Soda (Baking Soda)
- 1 tsp Vanilla Extract
- 150g (¾ Cup, packed) Light Brown Sugar
- 2 UK Large (US Extra Large) Free Range Eggs
- 75g ($^2/_3$ Stick) Butter, at room temperature + extra for greasing
- 175g (1¼ Cups) chopped, stoned Dried Dates
- 35g ($^1/_3$ Cup) Pecan Halves, chopped
- Pinch of Sea (Kosher) Salt

Sauce Ingredients

- 150g (¾ Cup, packed) Light Brown Sugar
- 100g (1 Stick less 1 tbsp) Butter, at room temperature
- 90ml (6 tbsp) Double (Heavy) Cream
- 35g ($^1/_3$ Cup) Pecan Halves, chopped

Serves: 8   Ready In: 40 mins

Note: If you are unable to source Chestnut Flour, just replace with gluten-free flour blend.

Directions

Preheat the oven to 160C fan, 350F, Gas Mark 4. Grease 8 individual pudding basins and place on a baking sheet.

Roughly chop the pecan nuts and dates. Measure out 175ml (¾ Cup) of boiling water. Place the chopped nuts and dates in a bowl, sprinkle over the bicarbonate of soda (baking soda) and vanilla extract, then pour over the boiling water and set aside.

Cream together the butter and sugar in the mixing bowl of a stand or hand-held food mixer. Beat together really well, (this should take at least 5 mins and preferably 10 mins). Whilst the butter and sugar is beating, in a separate bowl, whisk together the flour blend, chestnut flour, cornflour/corn starch, baking powder, bicarbonate of (baking) soda, xanthan gum and salt.

Break the eggs into a jug and lightly whisk with a fork. Gradually beat the eggs into the creamed butter/sugar mix, until well combined. Add flour mixture and, on a very low speed, beat until combined. Pour in the nuts, dates and their soaking liquid. Beat again on low to fully mix (don't worry if it looks a bit of a mess at this point).

Divide the mixture between the pudding basins and bake in the oven for 25 mins.

Meanwhile, roughly chop the pecan nuts for the butterscotch sauce. Place the remaining ingredients in a saucepan. Five minutes before the puddings are ready, heat the saucepan over a medium heat, stirring until the sugar is fully dissolved. Bring up to simmer and cook 2-3 mins until the sauce is sticky and caramel brown. Set aside to cool for about 3 mins.

Meanwhile, remove the puddings from the oven. When the butterscotch sauce has cooled slightly, protect your hands from the heat then run a knife around the inside of the pudding basins. Turn the puddings out into individual bowls or onto plates and serve with the sauce spooned over the top.

Vanilla Poached Pears

GF DF NF OF V Ve YF

Ingredients

- 4 ripe but firm Pears
- 125ml (½ cup) Sweet White Wine
- 2 tbsp Natural Caster (Superfine) Sugar
- 1 Lemon
- 1 Vanilla Pod

Directions

You will need a saucepan or casserole (Dutch Oven) that is large enough to snugly hold the upright pears. You will also need to cut a circle of parchment paper that is the same size as your pan, and then cut out a small hole in the middle of the circle.

Whisk together the wine, 240ml (1 Cup) water and sugar into your pan/casserole over a medium heat. Split the vanilla pod in 2 and scrape out all the beautiful seeds. Add these to the saucepan along with the vanilla pod and the zest of the lemon.

Squeeze the juice of the lemon into a bowl. Peel each of the pears (taking care to retain the stem) and toss each pear in the lemon juice to prevent discolouration before moving onto the next one. Place the pears upright into the saucepan/casserole (Dutch Oven) and carefully cover with the circle of parchment paper. Bring up to the simmer, then poach gently for 15-20 mins until the pears are tender and cooked through.

Carefully remove pears from the pan with a slotted spoon, then increase the heat to high and rapidly boil the cooking liquid until it has reduced to a lovely syrup (about 5 minutes). Discard the vanilla pod, spoon the syrup over the pears. These lovely, versatile pears can be served hot or warm or cold, but whichever way you serve them, they are delicious.

Cooking for 1 or 2? Prepare & Store Meal Tip:

These poached fruits with keep for up to 5 days in a sealed container stored in the fridge.

Serves: 4   Ready In: 30 mins

MINT CHOCOLATE & RASPBERRY POTS

Ingredients

- 60g (2oz) gluten-free Dark Chocolate With Mint
- ½ tbsp Cocoa Powder, (Dutch Processed in the US)
- 1 UK Large (US Extra Large) Free Range Egg White*
- 90g (¾ Cup) Raspberries

- 1 tbsp Natural Caster (Superfine) Sugar
- 45ml Double (Heavy) Cream
- 2 Small Mint Leaves

Note: Please use reconstituted dry egg white (readily available in supermarkets) if serving this dessert to anyone who should not consume raw eggs.

Directions

Break the chocolate into small pieces and put in a large bowl placed over a pan of simmering water (without the bottom touching the water). Stir and remove the pan from the heat when the chocolate has fully melted. Leave to cool slightly. Using a stand or handheld food mixer, whisk the egg white to soft peaks. Add the sugar and whisk again to create a thick, glossy meringue. In a separate bowl, whip the cream into soft folds. Fold this into the cooled chocolate with a metal spoon or silicon spatula. Then add about one-third of the meringue and fold in. Finally add the remaining meringue mixture and continue to very gently fold in until fully incorporated.

Reserve 2 raspberries for decoration, divide the rest between 2 teacups or glasses, then spoon over the chocolate mousse. Pop into the fridge and chill for 4-6 hrs. Place a raspberry and mint leaf on top of each pots to serve.

Serves: 2   Ready In: 30 mins plus chilling time

HONEY-ROASTED FIGS WITH WALNUTS

Ingredients

- 4 Fresh Figs (105g / 4oz)
- 8 Walnut Halves
- ½ Orange
- 4 tsp Honey

- ¼ tsp Ground Cinnamon
- Pinch Freshly Grated Nutmeg
- 30ml (2 tbsp) Greek Yogurt
- ½ tsp Olive Oil

Directions

Preheat the oven to 180C, 375F, Gas Mark 6.

Roughly chop the walnut haves and mix in a small bowl along with the spices, honey, finely grated zest and juice of the ½ orange. Cut a cross in the top of the figs to half-way down and squeeze their bases to open them up into a flower shape. Grease a baking dish with the olive oil. Nestle the figs into the dish, cut side up. Spoon the honey walnuts evenly over the figs, then back in the oven for 15 mins. Remove from the oven and allow to stand for 2 mins. Divide the figs into 2 bowls and top with the yogurt.

Serves: 2   Ready In: 15 mins

Summer Fruits Crumble

GF DF NF V Ve YF

Ingredients

- 110g (¾ Cup + 1 tbsp) Gluten-Free Plain (All Purpose) Flour Blend
- 30g ($^1/_3$ Cup) Gluten-Free Rolled Oats
- 25g (1 tbsp + 2 tsp) Light Brown Sugar
- 60g (4 tbsp) Buttery Sunflower Spread
- 1½ tsp Vanilla Extract
- 1½ tbsp Maple Syrup
- 500g (4 Cups) frozen Summer Fruit Mix, defrosted
- ¼ tsp Olive Oil

Directions

Preheat the oven to 180C fan, 400F, Gas Mark 6. Grease a baking dish with the olive oil.

Start by making the Oat Crumble. In a stand or handheld food mixer, add the flour and the cold spread, divided into small pieces. Mix together with the paddle/k-beater until the mixture resembles breadcrumbs. Add the rolled oats and brown sugar, mix together. Pop into the fridge until required.

Place the fruit in a bowl. Drizzle over the maple syrup and vanilla extract and mix well to combine. Tip into the baking dish and cover with the chilled crumble mixture.

Bake in the oven until the fruit is tender and the crumble is golden brown for 25-30 mins for one large crumble. Remove from oven and allow to cool for 5 mins before serving.

Cooking for 1 or 2? Prepare & Freeze Tip:

Use freezer-safe heat proof ramekins to make individual crumbles. Cook initially for 15 mins. Cool completely, cover with kitchen film then either freeze or store in the fridge for up to 5 days. To reheat, thoroughly defrost and then bake in a preheated oven (160C fan, 350F, Gas Mark 4) for 15 mins until thoroughly heated and golden.

Serves: 4   Ready In: 35 mins

HONEYED RHUBARB COBBLERS

GF **NF** **V** **YF**

Ingredients

- 40g (½ Cup) Rolled Oats
- 40g (3 tbsp) Natural Caster (Superfine) Sugar
- 45g (¼ Cup) Light Brown Sugar (Packed)
- 55g (¼ Cup) Buttery Sunflower Spread
- 1 tsp Vanilla Extract
- 1 UK Large (US Extra Large) Free Range Egg
- ¼ tsp gluten-free Baking Powder
- ¼ tsp Xanthan Gum
- 1 tbsp Buttermilk
- 4 Cups (485g) Fresh Rhubarb
- 65g (½ Cup) Gluten-Free Plain (All Purpose) Flour Blend
- 2 tbsp Honey

Directions

Preheat the oven to 180C fan, 400F, Gas Mark 6.

Start by making the Cobbler. In a stand or handheld food mixer, beat together the buttery spread and sugars until pale and fluffy. Break the egg into a cup or small jug and give it a little whisk. Keeping the food mixer on a medium speed, add half off the egg, beat until well combined then add the remaining half along with the vanilla extract, and beat until combined.

Whisk together the flour, oats, xanthan gum and baking powder. Turn the food mixer down to low and beat in half of the flour mix, then add the tbsp of buttermilk followed by the remaining flour mix. Cover with kitchen film and pop into the fridge 30 minutes to chill and firm up.

Clean and trim the rhubarb, then cut into bite size pieces and divide amongst 4 ovenproof ramekins. Drizzle each ramekin with ½ tbsp of honey and give the fruits a little stir. Place the ramekins onto a baking sheet, then divide out the cobbler topping evenly. Bake for 30 minutes or until the fruit is tender and the cobbler is golden brown.

Cooking for 1 or 2? Prepare & Freeze Tip: Use freeze-able ramekins. Part-bake for 20 mins and then cool completely. Cover with kitchen foil and freeze. To reheat, thoroughly defrost and then bake in a preheated oven (160C fan, 350F, Gas Mark 6) for 15 mins until thoroughly heated and golden.

Serves: 4   Ready In: 1 hr

BERRYLICIOUS SUMMER PUDDING GF DF NF OF V Ve

Ingredients

- 8 Slices Gluten-Free Brown Bread (vegan if required)
- 225g (1½ Cups) Blueberries
- 300g (2 Cups) Strawberries
- 225g (1½ Cups) Blackcurrants
- 250g (2 Cups) Raspberries
- 110g (½ Cup) Natural Caster (Superfine) Sugar
- 1 Cinnamon Stick

Directions

Start by washing the fruits then gently dry on kitchen paper. Remove the blackcurrants from their stalks by firmly holding the tip of each stalk and then sliding it up between the prongs of a fork, the berries will pull off easily. Put the berries, sugar and cinnamon stick in a large saucepan over a medium heat and let them cook for about 3-5 minutes only (do not over cook). Remove from the heat and set aside to infuse whilst you prepare the pudding basin.

Line a 1.25l (5 cup) pudding basin with two pieces of overlapping kitchen film, allowing enough film to overlap the edges by about 15cm/6". Find a plate or saucer that will fit neatly just inside the top rim of the pudding bowl and something that you can use as a weight (tins of tomatoes/beans can be a handy choice).

Cut the crusts off the bread. Dipping into the fruit compote, place 1 in the bottom of the pudding basin and then continue to dip the bread to line the sides of the basin, trimming as necessary, overlapping the slices to ensure that there are no holes and making sure that you have enough bread left to create a top. This pudding is meant to look rustic, rather than pretty, so don't be worried about cutting uneven shapes to create a fully lined bowl.

Measure out about 150g/²/₃ Cup of the fruit compote and put into a sealable container along with the cinnamon stick. Seal and put into the fridge until ready for serving. Pour the remaining fruits into the lined pudding basin. Fully cover the pudding with the remaining dipped bread. Bring cling film up and loosely seal. Put the plate or saucer on top and weight down with the cans. Pop into the fridge and chill for 6 hrs or overnight.

Just before serving the pudding, open out cling film then put a serving plate upside-down on top and flip over. Spoon the reserved compote all over, taking care to soak any bits of bread that still look white.

Cooking for 1 or 2? Prepare & Store Meal Tip: Summer Pudding will keep for 2-3 days in a sealed container stored in the fridge.

Serves: 6   Ready In: 30 mins plus chilling time

Dairy-Free Cinnamon Pear Parfaits

 GF DF NF OF V Ve YF

Ingredients

- 1 Ripe Pear
- 1 tbsp Maple Syrup
- ½ Vanilla Bean Pod
- ½ Lemon
- ½ Cinnamon Stick
- ½ tsp Ground Cinnamon
- 120g (½ Cup) Dairy-Free Yogurt
- Pinch freshly Ground Nutmeg

Directions

Using a vegetable peeler or sharp knife, cut a thin piece of peel (no pith) from the lemon half. Peel, core and quarter the pear, then cut each quarter into 3 slices. Place the pear slices into a saucepan, along with the piece of lemon peel, the juice of the ½ lemon, maple syrup and cinnamon stick. Split the ½ vanilla pod in half length wise, scrape out the seeds and add these and the pod to the pan. Give everything a good stir and over a gentle heat, bring up to the simmer. Simmer for 5-10 mins or until the pears are tender. If making in advance, remove to a sealable container, otherwise just set aside and allow to cool.

When ready to serve, whisk together the yogurt with the ground cinnamon. Then divide half of the pear compote between 2 serving glasses, followed by half of the cinnamon yogurt and then repeat. Top with a drizzle of any remaining pear compote syrup and a sprinkling of freshly grated nutmeg.

Note: Note – the pear compote can be made in the morning, stored in the fridge, which will allow the flavours to fully develop.

Serves: 2   Ready In: 30-35 mins

Pecan Streusel Stuffed Maple Peaches

Ingredients

- 3 large, firm, just ripe Peaches
- 65g ($^1/_3$ Cup + 1 tbsp) Gluten-Free Plain (All Purpose) Flour Blend
- 4 tbsp Gluten-Free Rolled Oats
- 1 tbsp Light Brown Sugar
- 40g (3 tbsp) Buttery Sunflower Spread
- 3 tsp Maple Syrup
- 2 tbsp Pecan Halves

Directions

Preheat the oven to 160C fan, 350F, Gas Mark 4.

Start by making the Pecan Streusel. Roughly chop the pecan halves. In a stand or handheld food mixer, place the flour and cold spread, divided into small pieces. Mix together with the paddle/k-beater until the mixture resembles breadcrumbs. Add the rolled oats, chopped pecans and brown sugar, mix together.

Halve the peaches and remove the stone. Place in a baking dish, cut side up. Drizzle ½ tsp of maple syrup over each peach half. Divide the streusel mixture over the halves, mounding them up.

Bake in the oven until the fruit is tender and the streusel is golden brown (about 30 mins). Remove from oven and allow to cool for 5 mins. Serve hot or warm.

Cooking for 1 or 2? Storage Tip:

Cook initially for 20 mins. Cool completely, transfer to a sealable container and store in the fridge for up to 4 days. Reheat in a preheated oven (160C fan, 350F, Gas Mark 6) for 15 mins until thoroughly heated and golden.

Serves: 4-6   Ready In: 30 mins

Dairy-Free Almond, Apricot & Amaretto Rice Pudding

Ingredients

- 125g (²/₃ Cup) Brown Basmati Rice (dry weight)
- 8 Ready-to-Eat Dried Apricots
- 2 tbsp Flaked Almonds
- 480ml (2 Cups) Unsweetened Almond Milk
- 2 tbsp Amaretto Liqueur
  eg Disaronno (optional) or Orange Juice

- 1½ tsp Vanilla Extract
- 1 Vanilla Pod
- Pinch Freshly Ground Nutmeg
- 1 Cinnamon stick
- 2½ tbsp Natural Caster (Superfine)

Directions

Dice the apricots and place in a small bowl. Cover with the Amaretto liqueur, toss and set aside to soak whilst the rice cooks. If you don't have Amaretto liqueur, you could use Cointreau or Grand Marnier, or alternatively, if you don't want to use alcohol, then soak in orange juice.

In a medium saucepan, combine the rice with 320ml (1 1/3 Cups) of cold water. Bring to boil, reduce the heat to low. Leaving the pan uncovered, simmer until most of the water has been absorbed (10-15 mins), but the rice remains a little wet.

Split the vanilla pod and scrap out the seeds. Add the seeds and the whole pod to the rice along with almond milk, sugar, vanilla extract, freshly ground nutmeg and cinnamon stick and give everything a good stir. Return to a simmer and cook, uncovered, for a further 20-25 mins, stirring occasionally.

Meanwhile, heat a sauté pan over a medium heat and toast the flaked almonds for 2-3 mins until golden. Remove immediate from the pan and add to the apricots.

This pudding can be served hot or cold.

If serving hot, once cooked, remove the cinnamon stick and vanilla pod, spoon into warm serving bowls then drizzle over a portion of soaked apricots and almonds.

If serving cold, transfer to a sealable container, allow to cool then seal and put into the fridge to chill. Then serve as above.

Cooking for 1 or 2? Prepare & Store Meal Tip:

This rice pudding will keep for up to 3 days in a sealed container stored in the fridge.

Serves: 4   Ready In: 1 hr Plus optional chilling time

Individual Ginger, Lemon & Blueberry Swirl Cheesecakes GF NF V YF

Ingredients

- 15g (1 tbsp) Butter + extra for greasing
- 2oz (60g) Gluten-Free Oat Biscuits Eg Nairns
- ½ tsp ground Ginger
- 245g (1 Cup + 1 tbsp) Soft Cheese
- 100g (½ Cup + 1 tbsp) Greek Yogurt
- 75g ($^1/_3$ Cup) Natural Caster (Superfine) Sugar
- 1¼ tbsp Corn starch/Cornflour
- 1 Lemon, divided
- 1 tsp Vanilla Extract
- 2 UK Large (US Extra Large) Free Range Eggs
- 35g (¼ Cup) Blueberries
- 1 tbsp Honey

Directions

Preheat the oven to 140C fan, 300F, Gas Mark 3.

In a sealed freezer bag, crush the oat biscuits into fine crumbs using a rolling pin, then mix in the ground ginger. Give the crumbs and ground ginger a good toss to combine. In a saucepan over a low heat, melt the butter spread. Pour in the crumbs and stir well to ensure that all the crumbs are coated with spread. Grease 4 ovenproof ramekins each with a little butter. Divide the buttery crumbs evenly amongst the ramekins and press down to form a firm base. Place onto a baking sheet and bake for 8 mins. Remove from the oven and set aside to cool. Increase the heat of the oven to 160C fan, 350F, Gas Mark 4.

Cut the lemon into two, but divide it into ¾ and ¼, not half and half. Wrap the quarter in kitchen film and put into a sealable plastic container along with 4 blueberries. Seal closed and pop into the fridge until ready to serve. Finely zest the remaining lemon and then, separately, juice the lemon. Set aside.

Next make the blueberry compote. In a small saucepan, combine the remaining blueberries with the honey, ½ tsp of lemon zest and 1 tsp of lemon juice. Over a medium-low heat, bring up to simmer, reduce heat to low and give simmer for 2-3 mins, giving it an occasional stir. Once cooked, stir rigorously to fully break down the fruit and set aside to cool.

Using a stand or handheld food mixer on low speed, beat the soft cheese and yogurt until smooth. Turn the speed to low and gradually add the caster (superfine) sugar. Scrape down the sides of the bowl. Break the eggs into a jug and whisk together the vanilla extract. Dissolve the cornflour (corn starch) in the remaining lemon juice. Slowly whisk the eggs into the creamed cheese mix, followed by the corn starch/cornflour slurry and finally the remaining lemon zest. The mixture will be quite runny but should be completely smooth.

You are now going to pour the filling over the crumb base, and it may be easier for you to do this by transferring the cheesecake mix into a jug. Divide the cheesecake mix evenly over the ramekins. Give each ramekin a light tap to remove any air bubbles.

Using a teaspoon, drizzle the blueberry compote into a swirl over the top of each cheesecake. If you want to get really fancy, use a toothpick to feather out and ripple the compote.

Transfer the ramekins into a roasting tin. Boil the kettle and very carefully pour boiling water into the roasting tin to reach half way up the sides of the ramekins, taking care not to splash boiling water onto the cheesecakes. Protecting your hands from the heat, place into the oven and bake for 10 mins, then lower the heat to 90C Fan, 225F, Gas Mark ¼. Bake another 15 mins. After the 15 mins, check the cheesecakes. They are done when the cheesecakes are set but still slightly wobbly in the centre. When they are cooked, turn off the oven, leave the door slightly ajar and leave for 1 hr, then transfer the individual ramekins to cool rack and cool completely, then chill in the fridge for at least 2 hrs or overnight.

To serve, cut three slices from the reserved lemon quarter and cut each slice into quarters. Place 3 lemon quarters and 1 blueberry on top of each of the cheesecakes.

Cooking for 1 or 2? Prepare & Freeze Tip:

Cook the cheesecakes in freeze-able ramekins or bake in cupcake wrappers in a muffin tin. After cooking and cooling, cover the ramekins with kitchen foil and freeze. Defrost thoroughly before serving.

Serves: 4   Ready In: 1 hr   plus chilling time

Blackberry Bakewell Sponge Puddings GF OF V YF

Ingredients

- 50g (¹⁄₃ Cup) Gluten-Free Plain (All Purpose) Flour Blend
- 8g (1 tbsp) Cornflour/Corn starch
- 65g (¹⁄₃ Cup) Natural Caster (Superfine), divided
- 45g (3 tbsp) Butter, at room temperature + extra for greasing
- 25g (3½ tbsp) Ground Almonds
- 1 UK Large (US Extra Large) Free Range Egg
- 1 tsp gluten-free Baking Powder
- ¼ tsp Bicarbonate of Soda (Baking Soda)
- ¼ tsp Xanthan Gum
- 4 tsp Sour Cream
- 235g (2¹⁄₃ Cups) Blackberries

Directions

Preheat the oven to 160C fan, 350F, Gas Mark 4.

In a bowl, mix together the blackberries with 4 tsp of the sugar. Divide between 4 heat-proof ramekins or put into 1 baking dish.

In a stand or handheld food mixer, beat together the remaining sugar with the butter until light and fluffy (this should take 5 mins). Break the egg into a small jug and lightly whisk, then add half to the mixing bowl and beat into fat/sugar mixture. When thoroughly combined, add the remaining egg and beat again.

Sieve together the flour, cornflour/corn starch, xanthan gum, baking powder and soda. With the food mixer on low, slowly add the flour, followed by the sour cream and finally the ground almonds. Make sure the mixture is thoroughly combined but don't over beat. Spoon the almond sponge mixture over the blackberries.

Bake in the oven (25 mins for one large sponge or 20 mins for 4 individual desserts).

Cooking for 1 or 2? Storage Tip:

Store in the fridge covered in kitchen film for up to 4 days. Alternatively, use freeze-able ramekins. Part-bake for 15 mins and then cool completely. Cover with kitchen foil and freeze. To reheat, thoroughly defrost and then bake in a preheated oven (160C fan, 350F, Gas Mark 6) for 15 mins until thoroughly heated and golden.

Serves: 4   Ready In: 30-35 mins

MAPLE APPLE & BLACKBERRY CRISPS GF DF V Ve YF

Ingredients

- 1 Medium Firm Eating Apple eg Cox, Braeburn, Fuji
- $^1/_3$ Cup (50g) Blackberries
- 4 tbsp gluten-free Rolled Oats
- 4 tsp (19g) Buttery Sunflower Spread
- 3 tbsp Maple Syrup, divided
- ½ tsp Vanilla Extract

Directions

Preheat the oven to 180C, 375F, Gas Mark 6.

Rinse, drain and pat dry the blackberries, put into a heat-proof bowl. Peel and slice the apple and add to the bowl along with 1 ½ tbsp of Maple Syrup. Divide between 2 heat-proof ramekins.

Without rinsing out the bowl, put in the buttery spread. Melt the spread either by placing in the microwave for 10 seconds at a time or by placing over a saucepan of boiling water. When the spread is melted, stir in the remaining maple syrup, vanilla extract and rolled oats. Mix well. Pile the oat crisp mix on top of the fruits and pop the ramekins into the oven for 25 mins. Serve hot, warm or cold.

Serves: 2   Ready In: 35 mins

Coconut Pumpkin Meringue Pots

Ingredients

- 65g (Scant ⅓ Cup) Natural Caster (Superfine) Sugar
- 2 tbsp Maple Syrup
- 120ml (½ Cup) Coconut Milk
- 165g (⅔ Cup) Pumpkin Puree
- 2 UK Large (US Extra Large) Free Range Eggs, divided
- 4 tsp Flaked Almonds
- ½ tsp Vanilla Extract
- ½ tsp Ground Cinnamon
- ¼ tsp Freshly Grated Nutmeg
- ¼ tsp Ground Ginger
- 2 tsp Cornflour (Corn starch), divided
- ¼ tsp White Wine Vinegar
- ¼ tsp Olive Oil

Note: Please use reconstituted dry egg white (readily available in supermarkets) if serving this dessert to anyone who should not consume raw eggs.

Directions

Preheat the oven to 180C fan, 350F, Gas Mark 6. Lightly grease 4 ovenproof ramekins with the olive oil. Place the ramekins into a roasting tin.

If you are unable to source canned pumpkin (not pumpkin pie mix), simply peel and chop about 200g of pumpkin or squash and then steam for 30 mins or until soft and tender. Then puree in a blender or food processor and cool slightly. Weigh out 165g ($^2/_3$ Cup).

Heat the coconut milk in a small saucepan over medium heat until scalding. Reduce heat to a low simmer and keep milk warm. Separate one of the eggs and set aside the white until later. Place the yolk in a large jug along with the all of the other egg, the maple syrup, vanilla extract, cinnamon, freshly grated nutmeg, ginger and 1 ½ tsp of cornflour (corn starch). Whisk everything together until well combined. Add the pumpkin and whisk again. Finally, keep whisking and pour over the hot coconut milk, whisking all the time until thoroughly combined.

Pour the pumpkin custard evenly into the ramekins. Boil the kettle and very carefully pour boiling water into the roasting tin to reach half way up the sides of the ramekins, taking care not to splash boiling water onto the pumpkin custards. Protecting your hands from the heat, place the custards into the oven and bake for 30 mins.

Meanwhile, using a stand or hand held food mixer, whisk the egg white until it forms stiff peaks. Keep whisking and add the sugar, until glossy and stiff. Finally add the ¼ tsp each of cornflour (corn starch) and white wine vinegar and whisk until combined.

After the initial 30 mins of cooking, remove the roasting tin from the oven and pile the meringue on top of the pumpkin custards to cover them completely. Fluff up the meringue into peaks. Scatter over the flaked almonds. Return to the oven for 12 minutes until the meringue is puffy and golden. Serve immediately.

Cooking for 1 or 2? Prepare & Store Meal Tip:

These pudding will keep for up to 2 days in a sealed container stored in the fridge.

Serves: 4   Ready In: 1 hr

TIRAMISU

Ingredients

- 12 Vanilla Drops*
- 1 tbsp Instant Coffee Powder/Granules
- 2 tbsp Amaretto Liqueur
- 230g (1 Cup) Mascarpone Cheese
- 240ml (1 Cup) Greek Yogurt
- 1½ tsp Vanilla Extract
- 3 tbsp Maple Syrup
- 1½ tsp Cocoa Powder

Directions

In a shallow bowl, dissolve the coffee in 2 tbsp (30ml) boiling water and stir in the Amaretto Liqueur. Set aside.

In a bowl, whisk together the mascarpone cheese, vanilla extract and maple syrup until light and airy, then fold in the Greek yogurt. Put the Vanilla Drops on a plate.

In each of 4 glasses or sundae dishes, spoon in 2 tbsp of the creamy mix. Sprinkle four of the Vanilla Drops with the coffee/amaretto mix and pop into the glass (you'll need to work quickly, as the sponges will go soggy quickly). Repeat twice more with another layer of creamy mix then soaked sponges. Finally, divide the remainder of the creamy mix between the four glasses. Chill for at least 30 mins before serving, dusting the top of each glass with ¼ tsp of cocoa powder when ready to serve.

Note: Use the Vanilla Drops Recipe on page 49 of this cookbook.

Serves: 4   Ready In: 15 mins plus chilling time

English Raspberry Trifle

Ingredients
- 6 Vanilla Drops*
- 250g (2 Cups) Fresh Raspberries
- 3 US Large (UK Medium) Free Range Egg Yolk
- 3 tbsp Natural Vanilla Caster (Superfine) Sugar*, divided
- 1½ tbsp Corn starch/Cornflour
- 120ml Double (Heavy) Cream
- 360ml (1½ Cups) Milk
- 2 tbsp Flaked Almonds
- 1 tsp vanilla extract
- 1 Vanilla Pod

Directions

In a bowl, sprinkle 1½ tbsp of vanilla sugar over the raspberries and set aside to macerate. In a heat-proof jug, whisk together the egg yolks with the corn starch/cornflour, remaining caster sugar, vanilla extract and 6 tbsp of milk. Heat the remaining milk in a small saucepan until it reaches scalding point (this is when bubbles start to appear around the edge of the pan before the milk boils). Whisk eggy mixture again to slacken it, then still whisking, first add 2 tbsp of hot milk, then whisk in the remainder. Return the custard the saucepan, and keeping whisking, cook over a gentle heat until it thickens. Remove from the heat quickly and pour back into the jug. Cover with kitchen film directly in contact with the custard (to prevent a skin from forming) and allow to cool.

Note: Use the Vanilla Drops Recipe on page 49 of this cookbook. Vanilla Sugar is natural caster sugar that has been stored with old vanilla pods, which impart a subtle vanilla flavour to the sugar. You can just substitute with caster (superfine) sugar if required.

Meanwhile, take 6 tbsp of the macerated raspberries and either mash with a fork or blitz in a mini-food processor. Spread both sides of the Vanilla Drops with raspberry purée. Divide the remaining raspberries between 4 glasses or sundae dishes, top each with 1½ Vanilla Drops and any remaining purée, then divide over the cooled custard and again cover each trifle with kitchen film in direct contact with the custard. Chill for at least 1 hr. Meanwhile, heat a non-stick sauté pan over a medium heat and add the flaked almonds. Watch them like a hawk, tossing very now and then, until the almonds are toasted and golden. Remove immediately to a saucer to cool. When ready to serve the trifles, in a clean bowl whip the cream until thickened and holds it shape. Remove the kitchen film and spoon over each trifle then scatter with the flaked almonds.

Serves: 4   Ready In: **30 mins** plus chilling time

RESOURCES & FURTHER INFORMATION

Gluten-Free Ingredients

Health Food Stores with a wide range of Gluten-Free Ingredients

US – www.traderjoes.com   UK – www.hollandandbarrett.com

Gluten-Free Flours & Other Baking Ingredients

US - www.wellbees.com, www.honeyville.com,   UK – www.dovesfarm.co.uk,
    www.bobsredmill.com   www.shipton-mill.com/flour-direct-shop

Masa Harina Flour

US – www.bobsredmill.com, www.amazon.com   UK - www.mexgrocer.co.uk, www.amazon.co.uk

Worcestershire Sauce

US – Gluten-free versions are widely available   UK - www.gluten-freeshop.co.uk, www.amazon.co.uk

Vegetarian Suet

US - n/a   UK - www.steenbergs.co.uk, www.amazon.co.uk

A NOTE FROM THE AUTHOR

Your Feedback

Thank you for choosing my Cookbook. I would love to know what you think of the recipes in this book, are any particular favourites? I would be most grateful you were able to leave a book review on the website that you purchased it from.

Further Gluten-Free Books & Bonus Free Giveaway

If you have enjoyed the recipes in this cookbook, you may also be interested in further books in this series:

Gluten Free & Wheat Free Diet Brunch & Breakfast Recipes Cookbook.

Your Bonus Gluten Free & Wheat Free FREE Giveaway

As a special Thank You to my readers, I have available an exclusive & free special bonus. Sign up for my Readers Group Newsletter and receive a FREE copy of the Gluten Free & Wheat Free Vegetarian Snacks Recipe Booklet.

To receive your free PDF copy of this booklet, you just need to visit http://goo.gl/Km3H1K and let me know where to email it to.

Let's Stay Connected

Please do also take a look at my author blog:

WWW.MILLYWHITECOOKS.COM

As well as details on my full range of cookbooks, you will also find articles and information on:

- Ingredients
- Cooking Techniques
- Equipment
- Health News
- Nutrition Information
- Special Offers

Every month I share a new menu of the month, showcasing recipes from my collection.

You can also find me on social media too:

 MillyWhiteCooks.com   facebook.com/MillyWhiteCooks

 pinterest.com/MillyWhiteCooks   instagram.com/MillyWhiteCooks

 twitter.com/MillyWhiteCooks   plus.google.com/+MillywhitecooksBooks/posts

INDEX

15942129R00044

Printed in Great Britain
by Amazon